edited
by
DEBBIE MARSHALL

Big Enough Dreams

photographs by
YVONNE DUBOURDIEU

 Learning Community Press, 2006

Book Copyright © 2006 The Edmonton Learning Community

Essays Copyright © the authors

Cover image: Davey Thompson

Cover and Interior Design: Jackie Boyko, Credo Young Enterprises

Copy Editor: Heather Marshall

Printed and bound in Canada by Priority Printing

Published in Canada by
The Learning Community Press

The Edmonton Learning Community is a network of self advocates,
parents, service providers, government employees, and educators interested
in promoting positive images of people with developmental disabilities.
The Learning Community believes that all people have strengths, skills and
gifts that contribute to the vitality of our communities. The intent of the
Learning Community is to create the time and space for ongoing learning
opportunities that influence a cultural shift in how supports are provided
to adults with developmental disabilities.

 We acknowledge the support of a Community
Capacity Building Grant from Edmonton Persons with
Developmental Disabilities (PDD) Community Board.

LIBRARY AND ARCHIVES CANADA CATALOGUING IN PUBLICATION

ISBN 0-9781739-0-2

In Memory of Carol Ann

Contents

Discounted annuals iii
Alice Major

Preface v
Gary McPherson

Introduction vii
Debbie Marshall

Exquisitely Abled 1
Myrna Kostash

Doing Lunch with John Benes 7
Cheryl Mahaffy

A Welcoming Spirit 19
Christine Wiesenthal

A Special Kind of Love 29
Dan Rubinstein

Big Enough Dreams 39
Michelle Ponich

The Blue Folder 45
Lorie Miseck and Beverly MacKinnon

The Director 53
Todd Babiak

Dancing Apart 59
Caterina Edwards

An Expressive Life 65
Gary Holdgrafer

Sidelining 71
Allison Kydd

Plus More 79
Gloria Sawai

The Cat's Meow 87
Mark Kozub

Two Steps Forward 95
Kalin Jensen

Here Comes Trouble 101
Shirley Serviss

Live Well, Laugh Much, Love Often................................109
Debbie Marshall

Taming the Triggers 115
Gayle Simonson

Tugboat Annie..121
Sophie Lees

At Twenty-Seven: Dean Kirkby's Story 129
Christie Schultz

My Ears, Joe's Tongue, Ryan's Finger, Jackie's Throat, Erik's Heart........137
Kalin Jensen

Launching Into Life...143
Allan Chambers

An Irrepressible Imp 149
Heather Boyd

No Holding Back 157
Debby Waldman

Just Trying to Make a Difference 165
Curtis Gillespie

An Obsession for Life 171
Susan Ruttan

Mister In-Between 179
Heather Marshall

The Perfect Blue 185
Allan Chambers

Springtime for Brent 193
Mark Haroun

The Love Between Them 199
Linda Goyette

Away from the Edge..207
Debbie Marshall

Contributors 217

Acknowledgments 229

Discounted annuals

By Alice Major

The big-box grocery is an acreage of cars
crowded round
a vast interior maze—towering
aisles and piles
of cans. A factory stocked and re-stocked by
unnoticed hands.

I meet Larry at the back, near the deli counter.
Where we can buy
a slice of pizza for a dollar eighty-five
and bottled juice.
Then Larry leads me surely through the maze,
taking our lunch
out of the air-conditioned chill that's good
for groceries.

Hi, Larry, says the girl who shoves a trolley
wobbling high
with cereal boxes. And, *How's it going, Larry?*
asks the greeter
who has to check for evidence we've truly paid
for our pizza.
Great day for the race, the greeter jokes.
The human race,
he adds. He's told this one before.

Outside there's a temporary garden—
discounted annuals
and bags of potting soil. Beyond it,
a picnic table
baking in reflected heat from stucco walls
and softening asphalt
where we open up our sponge-foam boxes.

Yes, Larry is a little different from the rest of us.
Somehow
his brain gets tagged with a discount sticker
by a world
that doesn't notice much beyond the check-out counter.

For other shoppers, this giant store is just
a passageway
through a random aggregation of
'have a nice days.'
But Larry knits it into a living village
where some folks
piss him off and many are his friends.

He stops to chat
with the pretty girl in the garden shop.
I buy a pot
of frilled petunias, amazing in their ordinary
luminosity.
Larry carries my new flowers to the car for me.
It's a great day
for the human.

Preface

A friend of mine once told me that a person could never have "big enough dreams." That friend was Rick Hansen, and he made this comment to me during the final stages of his *Man in Motion* trek in which he literally wheeled his wheelchair around the world. According to Rick, big dreams give people hope and a future to aspire towards. It also gives them a mental picture of what may be possible in their lives. I think the collection of stories that you are about to read is going to demonstrate this in spades.

When we care about someone, we have a tendency to want to protect them from being hurt. This so often happens when someone reveals their personal dreams to others who care about them (like close family and friends). When this happens, I call it unintended and inadvertent "dream stealing" or "dream killing," and this seems to be true, even if this concern is well-intended for the individual that is perceived to need protection from some unknown future.

Fortunately, many of the people in this anthology have been able to pursue their dreams and withstand that kind of overprotection. Others have also received timely encouragement that they may have needed from family, friends or someone else who cared about them. These stories are heart-warming and informative. They may even have the effect of forcing readers to re-evaluate biases and personal prejudices that they might hold.

Naïveté and personal fears are usually born out of a lack of exposure to situations, cultures, religions or people that may appear to be different than that to which we have normally become accustomed. I am convinced that by the time you finish reading this collection of outstanding personal stories you will recognize many situations where this may have occurred to you, or to others that you may know.

My experience of living with a disability since the age of nine after having contracted respiratory quadriplegia as a result of polio, has taught me that each one of us can learn something from anyone and everyone that we meet. However, this is only true if we take the time to listen, understand and engage others in a meaningful way. As I read these stories, I continued to add to my knowledge and understanding of humankind. I am sure that this book will do the same for you.

Gary McPherson C. M., LLD

Introduction

When I was a child in the mid-1960s, there was a store called Andy's on the corner of the working class street where I lived. Inside the shop were newspaper racks and wooden shelves lined with cheap toys, sugar and flour, boxes of Spic 'N Span and cartons of cigarettes. Along one wall was a dirty brown linoleum-topped lunch counter where burly men with slicked-back hair hunched over 50-cent bacon and egg breakfasts. Next to the counter stood a Victorian-era glass-fronted case containing bins of candy. When Andy wasn't frying eggs, he would stand behind the case and kids would tell him how many mojos, caramels or Popeye candy cigarettes they wanted and he'd drop them into small, crisp, brown paper bags.

My younger brothers and I spent a lot of dimes in that store. The minute we'd get outside we would fill our mouths with sweet and sour candy, eager to avoid our mother confiscating what would more than likely "spoil our dinner." Standing on the hot tarmac driveway near the gas pumps (Andy's also served as the local gas station) we'd sometimes spot a little girl wheeling her tricycle near the back door of the shop. Her glossy brown pigtails almost covered her large hearing aid. She had freckly skin, round eyes and a lop-sided smile. Her name was Nancy and she was Andy's daughter. Everyone in the neighborhood knew that Nancy was "retarded." She didn't attend our local grade one class or play with the other kids. Nancy also didn't venture far from the tiny yard behind the store—in those bad old days she would have risked the teasing and shunning that was commonplace when it came to persons with developmental disabilities.

My family moved away from that neighborhood and on to the suburbs when I was eleven. Working on this book decades later, I think back to that earlier time and have a new appreciation for Nancy. I wonder what it was like for her to live hidden away from the neighborhood kids, shut out of relationships with what were certainly her peers. I am also curious about what happened to her when she reached adolescence and adulthood. Did she attend special classes? Did she dream about jobs, marriage and a life of her own? What was she able to achieve from within the confines of that neighborhood and those times?

Until relatively recently, such questions were rarely asked of people with developmental disabilities. They were seen as not really having dreams of their own—at least not dreams that had any likelihood of being fulfilled. They lived under the tight control of their families or the state, were checked into institutions or shut away at home, all in an effort to protect them and what's more, to protect society. Persons with developmental disabilities were seen as unpredictable, occasionally frightening, and therefore the objects of control. While they sometimes received compassionate care in government facilities, they almost always lost their independence and their dignity. In some cases, they also suffered isolation and abuse.

Roughly thirty years ago, all that began to change. Human rights movements of the late 1960s and 70s raised new questions about how society treated various groups. Society had become enlightened, and the practices of many institutions came under public scrutiny. The doors of government "homes" for the "mentally unfit" were suddenly opened. New organizations were established, designed to provide persons with developmental disabilities with jobs and services. Suddenly, they were visible in a way that they hadn't been before.

Despite those monumental changes and the ongoing efforts to integrate people with developmental disabilities into society, there are still things that need to be changed. The old baggage of misunderstanding that was so common when I was a child is still in evidence, even though many people with disabilities are living fulfilled lives and participating more actively in community life. How often do people still avert their eyes when an intellectually challenged person is accompanied onto a bus by a caregiver? Or how many times do people stop and speak to the man who lives independently in the supported-living apartment in their neighborhood? Uncomfortable about a physical or intellectual condition we don't understand, put off by physical ticks or a drooping mouth, we smile, nod, and move on as quickly as possible. Our fears of the unpredictable, the mentally different, lead us to symbolically and sometimes literally, cross to the other side of the street.

The intent of this book is to help move people with developmental disabilities away from the back door to the front door of our collective consciousness. The approach of the book is revolutionary. Traditionally, books about people with developmental disabilities have been authored by parents, caregivers, and health care professionals. The results have often been paternal, jargon-bound, or overly-sentimental biographies. *Big Enough Dreams* takes a different approach. Some of Alberta's finest authors—award-winning writers Myrna Kostash and Gloria Sawai, poets Lorie Miseck and Shirley Serviss, editors Dan Rubinstein and Heather Boyd, playwright Mark Haroun, novelist Caterina Edwards, journalists Linda Goyette and Todd Babiak and a host of others—have been invited to craft honest, compelling stories of complex individuals who live with a wide range of intellectual disabilities. These are not "insider" stories, but fresh perspectives on lives that have too often been overlooked.

Big Enough Dreams opens with a piece by Myrna Kostash describing the ways in which she once saw (or didn't see) those who lived with disabilities of all kinds. She charts the ways in which her perceptions have changed over time, shaped by relationships with people who have carved out meaningful lives despite daunting challenges. Her language is direct and graphic. Some may find this disturbing; but most will realize that she is offering an honest restatement of the ways in which many of us once thought of people with disabilities. The piece ends with a description of her recent encounters with a young woman whose friendship has made Myrna revisit and transform some of her own preconceptions about persons with developmental disabilities.

From there, the book's writers describe the new ways in which people with developmental disabilities are being seen. They also detail the changing realities facing these individuals. Dan Rubinstein, Sophie Lees, and Linda Goyette profile couples who have relationships, families, jobs and responsibilities. Mark Haroun, Kalin Jensen, Michelle Ponich, and Allan Chambers explore the lives of artists, labourers, waitresses, writers, jocks, actors, and musicians. All of the stories in this book describe people who are passionate, competitive, uptight, talkative, petty, beautiful, obsessive, silent, troubled, open-minded, mean-spirited, ambitious, hard-working, caring and funny. In other words, fully human.

People with developmental disabilities want and expect to be a fundamental part of society and are unwilling to go back into the institutional closet. They are real people with real hopes, and as the title of this anthology suggests, they have big dreams and are working hard to fulfill them.

Debbie Marshall

by
Myrna KOSTASH

Exquisitely Abled

You were born who you are, then came through it. I haven't passed that test....
If I do this right, I disappear—which leaves you here alone, among
these shadows on the face of reason.

(Bruce Rice, from "Frowning Girl," *The Illustrated Statue of Liberty*)

———————

When I met Jocelyn Bell and her parents, Denis and Kathie, as new neighbours in my condominium building, I would have said that she was the first person with a disability that I knew.

Now I must correct that claim: Jocelyn Bell is the first disabled person I have had as a friend. But the disabled have peopled my life since as far back as I can remember.

Uncle Elias had a bum left leg, fused at the knee joint to treat TB of the bone back in the 1930s, and for the rest of his life walked without being able to bend it, lurching sideways and swinging widely in order to get around the farm and his tasks. David, a boy in my Ukrainian dancing class, had a brain tumour removed. This left him blind, but he kept on dancing, head tilted slightly to the side, eyes hidden behind dark glasses, as we sighted dancers moved him gently around—there was nothing wrong with his legs—keeping him in position. There were two children in my elementary school born of the thalidomide scandal, with arms truncated below the shoulder and a finger-sprout for a hand. I do not remember if they were ever fitted with prosthetic limbs, but I do remember their bewildering cheerfulness in spite of their condition. Did they not mourn the phantom limbs that had never grown?

Elsewhere in that school there was a girl with an ugly and heavy black boot for a shoe, its sole several inches deep, propping up her shrivelled leg. Another girl had a cruel, metal frame—a brace—gripping a leg which had been disabled by the polio virus we were all terrified of succumbing to, like those pitiable creatures in the black and white photographs in *Life* magazine who were condemned to breathe out their lives inside an iron lung, a sinister canister wheezing through bellows, leaving the children with the one task they could fulfill: smiling for the cameras. Polio: a student teacher dragging his dead legs behind him as he thrust himself forward by means of wooden crutches rammed into his armpits. He had the neck and shoulders of a quarterback.

At university we all cheered on—if only from a discreet distance— the student in the wheelchair, afflicted by cerebral palsy, who nevertheless pulled his chair alongside ours in the classrooms and the libraries, heard the same lectures and read the same books while threshing about within his straps, his head jerking insistently to the left, knocking hard on the headrest.

An acquaintance's husband was diagnosed with Multiple Sclerosis. I watched the progress of the disease as I sighted him here and there, at Safeway's, on Whyte Avenue, at a bus stop, first walking merely with grim deliberation, one foot studiedly ahead of the other, dragging the other one along behind, scuffing the pavement, then walking with broad rotations of his torso, as though walking was now a feat of the musculature and synapses of his entire body. But I have not seen him now for a very long time. A neighbour's daughter was discovered to be deaf and the mother learned to sign while the rest of us smiled idiotically, saying "Hel-lo" with exaggerated stretches of our mouths. A friend's brother was diagnosed with schizophrenia and has since disappeared into obesity and nonsensical monologues.

I have seen amputees, empty shirtsleeves pinned up. I have seen legless beggars on homemade skateboards, pushing themselves along, weaving in and out of the human traffic on city sidewalks. I have seen middle-aged men and women with Down syndrome holding hands with their aged parents, waiting in line for a movie. I have watched caregivers push their charges swaddled in blankets along to a park, the young patient's groans, grimacing features and frantically-swerving eyes suddenly coming to rest as he lifted his face to the sun.

And then, some time early in the 1980s, I began to notice other things: the public telephone mounted at head-level for someone in a wheelchair, the enlarged washroom stall with the handrails, the dip in the sidewalk curb, the disabled-only parking stalls, the city buses lowering their steps to admit a passenger in a wheelchair, the loud beeping at intersections signalling the "go" light for pedestrians, the person onstage at a lecture, signing, the Braille numbers on elevator keypads…all of these items so stupendously civic-minded when compared with the norms in cities I was then travelling in (Warsaw, Athens, Kyiv, Bucharest, where disabled people were stranded in apartment buildings where elevators didn't work, the palsied were abandoned at hospital gates, and the blind left alone in the dark).

What was beginning to happen in Canada was the normalization of the citizen with disabilities. Society had finally recognized that the disabled—of mind and body—are everywhere among us, they share citizenship as well as humanity with us, and we can only experience that mutuality and collaboration if we enable it.

Which brings me back to Jocelyn.

In a sense it has been easy to get to know Jocelyn. Her parents have arranged for all the caregiving she needs, freeing me and others to be her friends (a distinction they have made clear) which has meant being included in family events like Thanksgiving dinners, Jocelyn's birthday parties and her graduation from high school, receiving Valentine's cards from her written by Kathie, and being greeted with a hug when I come through the door. But in another sense I do not know Jocelyn at all. She has a syndrome—the result of an incomplete gene—which has severely limited her intellectually, stunted her growth, and requires elaborate medication. The fact is that I have never had anything like a sustained conversation with her; Denis and Kathie "translate" for me. She is hard to understand on the phone and her mood swings can be bewildering. I know Jocelyn's body only as the waddling figure all dressed up for outdoors or the cuddly form in pyjamas ready for bed. So it is not so much about Jocelyn that I am able to write as it is about me—me as I think about Jocelyn.

I had not thought I knew any people with disabilities. But that is because, at least since I became an adult, I did not have any relationship with them. They were neither lovers nor close friends, nor family, and I had no responsibility for them. I was mildly interested in their welfare but otherwise made no further enquiries. I admired the gumption of people like Terry Fox and Rick Hansen and Heather McCartney, bought the Christmas cards designed by foot-and-mouth artists, and waived permission fees for work of mine reproduced by the CNIB. But they all disappeared into the category of "disability" (I could never make myself use the insufferably patronizing "differently-abled") as though the experience of the men and women themselves of their blindness or paralysis or derangement were generic: their only peculiarity was that they were not "normal."

But now I see, even from my limited perspective, that there is a Jocelyn-ness about Jocelyn's disabilities. Her wide-spaced eyes and her contorting mouth are very much *her* face, her sudden, fierce hugs are very much from *her* small body, her spasms of laughter are *her* expressed pleasure, and her almost-uncontainable excitement about a piece of music—music is Jocelyn's constant companion—and her growing absorption by the gestures of the Anglican Liturgy are *her* appropriation of beauty and even, who knows, of divinity.

I have no idea whether she has an apprehension of her condition, but *my* apprehension of it is that, thanks to her parents' decision to keep Jocelyn at home with them as long as possible or desirable (thanks in large part to the unflagging round of caregivers in her daily routine) Jocelyn, for all her disability, is part of a circle of intimacy and kinship, part of the story-telling and joking and kidding around within it, of nostalgia and memory across generations, including her own. The fact that I have been welcomed into all this—where a Jocelyn-smile can light me up—and that I make my way through it tentatively but hopefully, makes me think back on all those other people with disabilities whose paths I crossed one way or another. How I missed seeing what I see now when I'm in Jocelyn's company: human "normality" doesn't reside in individual brains and bodies but in the desire to be acknowledged by each other and scooped up into relationship.

Some of us, exquisitely abled, are better at this than others.

by
Cheryl MAHAFFY

Doing Lunch with John Benes

Walking into an Edmonton Tim Horton's, I'm on alert, scanning for a man who might be John Benes, Chief Volunteer Correspondent with Catholic Social Services. No sooner has the door swung shut than a likely candidate sidesteps past, angular face at an inquiring tilt. He circles out of earshot, so I turn instead to a woman near the front who'd been talking to him moments before. Perhaps this is Ella Zolotowska-Wyka, the outreach worker who promised to join us. "Are you waiting for someone?" I ask.

"No." The woman looks slightly harassed, and I realize that this must be her second baffling interruption in as many minutes. Of course she isn't Ella. Her table seats only two.

By now the real Ella is calling from across the restaurant and John Benes (that guess was right) and I converge at her table. "Get yourself a drink," John orders, close-cropped head bobbing somewhere between "yes" and "no," an involuntary gesture I soon recognize as uniquely his. "Get yourself a drink." He has decided how this meeting should go and step one is a coffee for me.

I've barely had time to learn that John has a vendetta against cigarettes and alcohol when a trio of transit security officers slide in beside us. "You guys do a good job, keeping people safe on the bus," John tells them. He recalls attending the recent grand opening of a new transit station to gather fodder for the newsletter that is his main contribution to the Edmonton scene. "It's a big job," he says—meaning transit security, not the newsletter. "Public safety is a number one issue."

Public transportation is John's main way of navigating from his Jasper Avenue apartment to the public and personal events that punctuate his days. "Do you ever feel unsafe riding transit?" I ask.

"Push me down the stairs," John responds, rocking, repeating. I strain to catch the words; perhaps it's "Pushing down the stairs." As the phrase cycles, a sprinkling of unrelated ideas suggests this may not be about feeling safe on transit, but about something deeper in his past.

The past is not a place to which John easily returns, but one day he allows me to send him back in time. Sorting through his staccato bursts of speech, I piece together a story that begins November 3, 1957 at Calgary Foothills Hospital. It involves multiple early tragedies: alcoholic parents, recurrent abuse, being orphaned at an early age, fetal alcohol syndrome (FAS).

As it turns out, not all of these memories are of real events. John does not have fetal alcohol syndrome, Ella tells me later. She wonders if he adds details like this to his life story in order to answer nagging questions about why he is the way he is. For instance, FAS may be his way of accounting for a brain that simultaneously gives him amazing recall and limited social savvy. There may also be another reason for John's embrace of FAS as part of his personal history; he is keenly aware of (and benefits from) available programs for adults with developmental disabilities and knows that FAS is attracting attention.

Most of John's story, however, rings true. In the early sixties, he lived with an Edmonton foster family and attended Winnifred Stewart School, a place ahead of its time in working with "unteachable" students. "My foster dad played the accordion, but he used to smoke heavy—pretty bad smoker," John says. After several moves, the family settled in a Westmount area home that John still passes when riding bus 133. "Fifth house down," he says. "That was the last home before I went to Red Deer."

Red Deer. That would be Michener Centre, the institution for persons once termed "mentally defective," where John spent much of the 1970s. As he recalls those years, one word recurs: abuse. "I got caught in that too," he says. "Wrong. So rampant and they couldn't stop it."

"Were there good things about your time there?"

"No." John shakes his head, definite. "I've gone through abuse. Over and over again. Never stopped. Never stopped." Later, when I tug him back to Michener, he recalls happier times: dances, movies, woodworking. Yet there's something about the name that continues to trigger talk of trouble and ill-treatment.

Like many relegated to the Centre, John did not belong there, says Father Brian Jayawardhana, a Catholic Social Services (CSS) counselor who specializes in intellectual disabilities. In May 1979, amid widespread reintegration of institutionalized people, an assessment at the Centre termed John "a good candidate for community placement" due to "good verbal and motor skills and abilities in perception, abstraction and organization."

By the end of the year, John had moved to Pineview, a west Edmonton residence run by the Good Samaritan Society. "Learning to ride the bus and everything," he says of that chapter in his life. "I used to be lost on the bus several times. After three years to learn, bus is better."

In 1981, John transferred to an east Edmonton apartment run by CSS, beginning a relationship with the agency that has spanned more than two decades. Soon he was out and about, gathering information and doing his best to share it with others. He would talk like a reporter, recalls Bev Oldham, a former night support worker in his complex. "He could be like a bull in a china shop, yet he knew so many things."

Seeing John's desire to communicate, Father Brian invited Bev to help John write his thoughts down. Thus began *John's News & Views*. Nearly twenty-five years later, the newsletter still comes out once a season, outlasting many publications with greater means. Father Brian says he gleans much of his knowledge about Edmonton goings-on from its pages. "I am a headline reader, but when I get John's newsletter, which is usually two or three pages, I read the entire thing. Now, how many others do that, I don't know. But if there are only two readers, they will have a synopsis of Edmonton news just by reading John's newsletter."

I'm sitting in Marc Barylo's office at CSS headquarters in south Edmonton, production central for *John's News and Views* since 1991. Given Marc's sensitive nature and John's penchant for stopping at every doorway whenever he's in the building, perhaps it's no surprise the two teamed up, says Father Brian. But Marc's job as CSS Director of Communications leans to such high profile responsibilities as the annual Sign of Hope fundraising campaign. Why did he agree to add John's newsletter to his list?

"Because John wants to tell the world about all the great things that are happening out there," Marc says. "And it's important for him as well. John loves people, he's proud of our city. This guy has a gift to offer, and it's his way of contributing."

"Can I drop by when you do the next issue?" I'm curious to see this duo in action.

"That may throw him off," Marc cautions. "We close the door, and he doesn't want any interruptions. He's come here to do work and that's his work."

Instead, Marc paints a verbal picture. "John will pull up a chair next to me, and I'll say, 'Okay, where do we start?' And he starts talking. He dictates to me." Out comes news about sporting events, grand openings, hotel renovations, hospital projects, civic happenings, social programs—complete with names, dates and numbers. "He doesn't forget a trick," Marc says. "If he does forget, it's because he never did know." I envision memory emerging intact as if from the bowl that pulls Harry Potter back in time.

Marc admits to making some changes as he types, but not many. "It usually takes about an hour and a half to dictate, and then I'll print it out and he'll check it. He's very complimentary; he'll say, 'Oh, that's good, how you put that.' He'll pick up spelling mistakes, and yet he can't write it all out. The way his brain processes is quite interesting."

The spring newsletter is two months away when I next see John. "May 25. That's the day. Most of the events are covered," he says. Already, his brain has cached most of this newsletter, including its production date.

I'm jealous, being notoriously weak in the art of remembering names and numbers. "That's amazing," I enthuse. "How do you do it?"

"The Lord helps me do that," he says. "The Lord helps me do that."

"Have you always been good at remembering?"

"Huh?" Often he doesn't understand a question or asks me to repeat. Catching my reply, he plays it back, and I sense that he's adding to his repertoire.

"Have you always been good at remembering?"

"Yeah. I go to deliver newsletters to different places." As often happens, the conversation takes an unexpected turn, and I scramble to keep up.

"So you do the distribution, too?"

"Yeah. Running around like a rubber chicken."

Marc confirms that John does most of the deliveries, although CSS faxes the newsletter to hotels and other downtown spots and makes copies available to staff. "So he runs a newspaper on his own, like a one-man show. He's just a man about town."

Among John's regular stops is the Downtown Business Association on Jasper Avenue. "He does give me a little newsletter, and once in awhile it actually tells me something I don't know," says DBA Information Coordinator Christine Watson, a chuckle in her voice.

Like many he visits, Christine is not sure how best to respond as John chats on rather aimlessly, wanders the halls in search of familiar faces and helps himself to any food in the staff kitchen. She has learned some things about him, including the fact that he'll respect a closed door. Yet she expects there's another layer to his personality. "He is one of those people I've wondered, 'Do we need to know a bit more about what his nature is, so I know the best way to manage his visit—and be respectful?'"

Beyond his informal walkabouts, John is a fixture at public celebrations where he regularly buttonholes the VIP of the day. "He's not backwards about coming forward to the main attraction," says Christmas Bureau Executive Director Wendy Batty, whose events attract a lineup of dignitaries. "What he says may be totally out of context, but it will be a timely issue. Then some switch will go on, and he's on to the next person."

John's motives are clear: "I go to grand openings so I can report in my newsletter, let everybody know what's going on and wish them well." But a gregarious nature combined with a certain lack of judgment can get a man in trouble. For a while, he was introducing himself as editor of the CSS newsletter, causing considerable confusion until Marc designed business cards to clarify the relationship. John has also been banned from certain sites for being too free with his hugs. "John, you've got to watch that sort of thing. You never know how they're taking it," Marc will tell him. Sometimes it seems to stick. Other times—not.

Yet it's remarkable how many Edmonton CEOs, hoteliers, nonprofit directors, mayors, police and fire chiefs not only know John by name but take time to chat and treat him to lunch. "I think his growth is a tribute, really, to their willingness to accept him and listen to him and be supportive of who he is," Marc reflects. "It's not like they condone certain behaviour just to get John off their back. They're very interested in him. They treat him with dignity and respect."

"Let's do lunch." It's a favourite phrase of John's, second only to "Let's have a party." *Doing lunch* is part of being a professional, a way to connect with clients and friends. Besides, John loves to eat—particularly potatoes and gravy. But be forewarned, you pick up the bill; being on an AISH (Assured Income for the Severely Handicapped) budget, John has little cash to buy his own lunches out.

Five years ago, Wendy Batty joined the ranks of Edmonton leaders who do lunch with John. Each year, during the Christmas Bureau's volunteer appreciation night, John sets the date while giving her his customary hug and holiday wishes. Without fail, the duo does lunch the third week in February at the Beverly Crest.

Months away from the next lunch date, Wendy can predict exactly how it will unfold. "Lunch is always at twelve, but I can almost set my watch that John will be here 11:30. He will want two cups of coffee—or if not that, two juices. He will sit at my desk and look for my tiny little radio. I listen to CBC but he changes to 630 CHED and turns it on precisely when the news will start. He turns one of the little speakers to me and the other to him, and when the news is over, he turns it off. I drive to the restaurant, we sit at the same table and nothing changes: the order we eat in, the volume he eats, the mess we leave behind. At the end, he says 'You go back to work now.' We walk out, he gives me a big hug, he goes over to catch the bus."

Even their conversation will follow a pattern, circling certain topics. "He is consumed by what he hears on the news, especially the negative; he will labour about that. But I don't know anything about *him*, because he doesn't tell you a darn thing. He could have been hatched for all I know, because he never speaks of any family." Nor does he talk about the fact that he's a regular

Christmas Bureau recipient, Wendy adds. I store that tidbit, wondering.

"He loves a good joke, and it's lovely to hear him laugh," Wendy says. "His eccentricity you almost find charismatic, because he's so unique."

On Tuesday afternoons John Benes is at Jubilee Lodge, getting snacks for the band of the day and wheeling residents into the dining hall to hear the music. It's one of the opportunities that came his way through Chrysalis, an organization he has been involved with since the early 1980s. He didn't stay long at other jobs, such as peeling avocadoes and working in a printing plant, but this volunteer gig has lasted fifteen years. These days, it's filling a need made more acute by staff shortage.

"Like a coffee?" he asks when I arrive to watch him at work. He dashes off to the staff room to fetch a cup, his uneven gait familiar by now, then resettles with his juice. Waiting to go on duty.

"Sad day. Woman died in bathtub. Have to live with for a long time. Won't be easy for anybody. Want to say a prayer that God gives them strength." I'm reminded that this is the lodge where a resident was scalded while being bathed. As usual, the downside of the news is on John's mind. A man on oxygen prompts another familiar theme: "Smoking. Damaged. Never want to be a smoker, eh? Tragic. Bad habit."

"How's the coffee?" he asks. And later: "Have trouble getting here?" He's a considerate host, if scattered.

Now it's time to wheel the residents from the elevator to their places at the table. "I have to go to work," he says, leading me to a bench. "Sit here and watch."

"I could help you."

"No. Just sit down and watch."

Later, seeing my notebook, he grabs one of his own, becoming my double as we commiserate with a recreation therapist about workloads. "We really appreciate John's help," she says. We both scribble, and I wonder if John can read his handwriting any better than I can read mine.

"Anything you'd like to add?" I ask.

"I always get compliments from the families," he says. "They appreciate the hard labour. It brings tears to the eyes, some of the families. They need to talk about something important, I'm there to help them."

John and Ella are outlining the supports that enable him to live alone: help with hygiene, laundry, medical appointments, finances, social outings and more. "I'm very fortunate to have good people to work with here," John says, and I realize belatedly that he is no longer speaking as one served, but as one who has helped Ella and others overcome nicotine and a host of other troubles. "[Ella is] doing a lot better now. Way better. Because I was there to help her out."

"How could you say that, John?" Ella splutters as he expands on the sorrows in her life while momentarily ignoring the ways that he has been helped by others. But his words march on: "I offer support. And that's important." It's clear that John prefers to stand on the helping end of the client-agency relationship.

Yet many people—including Ella—try hard to provide John with the support systems he needs in order to live an independent life. Realizing that John's involuntary rocking and bobbing adds to his difficulty in social settings, Father Brian recently recommended medication, but with disappointing results. Not only do John's ticks remain, but he has lost some of his smiling, happy go-lucky ways. "Maybe he should be slowly phased off, so we could get the real John back," Father Brian muses. "Sometimes I wish that I could have done more for John."

Despite such concerns, John has nothing but praise for the support he receives from Father Brian, Ella, and others. Perhaps his persistence in seeing himself simultaneously as a peer offers a life lesson. I recall other comments made by John during our conversation with Ella. "All of us have to support each other. All three of us in this room today. We have to support each other."

A Christian, John Benes wears his faith very publicly. "We pray together regularly. And I am not a religious person," says Wendy Batty. "He sits across the table, takes my hand and says, 'We'll say a prayer so the Lord will ensure the works of the Christmas Bureau.' And then he will go on and on with such clarity that it blows you away."

John traces his faith back to a particular time and place. "The Lord changed my life around at West Edmonton Mall chapel in 1988," he'll say. Soon after being baptized in mall waters, he began attending Central Pentecostal Tabernacle. "I met a lot of good friends over the years," he says. "Go out with parishioners, have lunch and fellowship with them. Enjoy. Just enjoy my time with them."

As I enter the Central Tabernacle foyer on a sunny Sunday, John is right in the thick of things, chocolate milk in hand. He breaks off from chatting to introduce me around. Inside the sanctuary, we sit in John's usual spot, centre front, and he makes sure to present me to Pastor Bob. "Right on," John says when a visiting speaker gives a long-ago Sunday School teacher a mustard seed necklace and a hug. "Beautiful." During a break in the action, he hurries over to the speaker for a quick personal word. Even when seated, he's never still.

Lawyer Martin Kemp is one parishioner who makes sure that John has a place to celebrate holidays—and of course they do lunch, three times a year. John has gained some social skills over the years, says Martin. "It used to be he'd find a new person, go overboard and they'd get scared off. Now he has the wisdom to try not to overdo it, so he can keep that relationship."

Christians who befriend John are simply doing what the Bible instructs, Martin adds—and it's not always about giving. He recalls a men's retreat in which John's denunciation of bad habits prompted a dramatic change of heart in a burly man who'd been "holding onto hate" for twenty years. "It just amazed me," recalls Martin. "You don't expect John to have a deep impact on someone's spiritual life. But in my faith, I believe that's the way God uses John Benes. And even if it is a relationship where I'm serving John more, there is a great benefit to me. In implementing selfless behaviour, I become a better person as well."

John feels deeply. He worried in 1994 when Father Brian had open heart surgery and was beside himself a decade later when Marc Barylo went through the same thing.

It's not always easy to be on the receiving end of that concern. A long-time target of John's anti-smoking crusade, Marc recalls the day he'd had enough. "Finally I said, 'You know, John, I'm your friend and I'll take care of your newsletter for you, but when it comes to smoking, mind your own business. I don't want to hear any more about it.'"

Not that John quit crusading. "Pray for Marc, that he'll quit smoking," he'd instruct other staff. But in Marc's presence, he limited himself to dark looks when the subject heated up.

"He respects that boundary, and I appreciate that," says Marc, who quit smoking prior to open heart surgery and isn't about to give John the satisfaction of linking that quitting to a crusade.

Nicotine aside, John's depth of feeling can be instructive, says Marc. "He's so excited about all the littlest things we just take for granted, and he's got childlike innocence that is quite beautiful to see. When you want to get through all the muck of bureaucracy and doublespeak, John's always there. And he can see with clarity, you know. He gets to the heart of the matter. So I learn a lot from him."

What does John wish for himself? A girlfriend. Several friends mention that desire, and he confirms it's true.

"Have you had girlfriends?"

"Yeah, I've had a few."

"They didn't stick around?"

"Not really."

"So what would you like in a girlfriend?"

"Just be with her. Get to know her and to have quiet time with her. Have that quiet time with her," he says. "I like somebody very tender. Like the song, Elvis. *Love me Tender*. That's my favourite love song. Elvis. 1956."

We're heading northeast up Edmonton's Fort Road, me in the driver's seat and John on alert. Guess what we're doing? Lunch.

It's soon clear John knows the rules of the road—and wants them followed. "Straight ahead. Wait for the light. Transit tracks." May as well be driving with my husband, I think, but then remember that John was knocked down while crossing the street not far from here about twenty years ago, fracturing his pelvis. Given his elephantine memory and tendency to worry, no wonder he's on alert.

The mug of milk I order later also strikes a chord, and John stretches an arm across to mime a milking of his outspread fingers into my pool of white. "Moo."

"Looks as if you know how to milk a cow," I hazard.

"I grew up on a farm." More of his past trickling out? If so, only a little. We may be here for a "working lunch," as John likes to say, but it's soon apparent that a march through his personal history is not on the agenda. We're here for fellowship. And eating heartily.

"Enjoying your meal?" he asks anyone walking past. "Good food?" Everyone gets high-fives; the waitress, other diners, me. "Great fellowship. You'll never forget this day. You'll tell your family about this fellowship." His generosity of spirit puts me to shame.

Over a third bowl of mushroom soup, John admits he went without breakfast, having no food in the house. What about the Meals on Wheels package that arrived at his apartment just before me? That'll be supper, he says. John was losing weight before Meals on Wheels entered his life, and I'm beginning to understand why.

Learning that his schedule for the week includes an opening of a 300-seat restaurant in the World Trade Centre downtown, I ask: "Can I come along?"

"No. Working."

"1:05 p.m.," he says. "That's when we'll leave the restaurant. Just enough time for coffee and dessert." John sticks with comfort food: three colours of gelatin with white stuff on top, a handful of sandwich cookies with white stuff in the middle.

I reach for a creamer and he takes it from my hand, a gleam in his eye. "Show you something," he says. Fork in hand, he pokes a row of holes in the top, poises the creamer above my coffee and squeezes out fingers of milk.

"Milking the cow again," I say, laughing. "I'll have to get you back for that."

He joins in, his laugh infectious. Pleased to have made me smile.

by
Christine WIESENTHAL

A Welcoming Spirit

As you drive northwest out of Edmonton, the commercial strip malls and car dealerships gradually thin out, giving way to more fields and pasture land, to horses grazing lazily in winter grasses and rural homes surrounded by tall shelter belts. Just before the French Catholic town of St. Albert, settled by missionaries in the nineteenth century, an exit road lined with mature pine and oak trees leads off across a swath of farmers' fields. Eventually, the road reaches the edge of a newer suburban subdivision, a place where the growing municipality of St. Albert nudges out to meet the Alberta prairie around it. A bedroom community of quiet cul-de-sacs and lanes lined with immaculately groomed two-storey homes, this tidy suburban enclave seems the picture of unremarkable middle-class comfort and ease. And if you were to stop before one of these white and brick homes, a house graced by a verandah and a triple garage with the requisite basketball hoop hanging over the driveway, you wouldn't notice anything distinctive or out of the ordinary, either. Even the hand-painted _Welcome_ sign that hangs from hooks by the front door would seem cozily familiar. You would never guess that behind this painted sign unfolds the story of a young woman who, despite her affluent surroundings, has never taken certain luxuries of comfort and ease for granted. Nor could you guess just how well this home-made sign's one word, _Welcome_, captures the generous and gracious spirit of this same young woman, who also happens to be the artist who painted it.

Welcome to the story of Jan Allard, a young woman of extraordinary courage and diligence in a seemingly ordinary world. She is a very busy young woman of multiple pursuits and various gifts—among them, an ability to help us see the world in remarkable ways, through her eyes.

"It's been a long journey, hasn't it, Jan?" Judy Allard muses, turning with a smile to her daughter. "Well, *we* remember it as a journey, likely not you."

Jan twists a strand of shoulder-length blonde hair and regards Judy with an open, trusting gaze, her lovely blue-grey eyes a carbon copy of her mother's. I am sitting with Jan and her parents, Judy and Jim, in their inviting family room. January sunshine spills in through the south-facing patio doors. The "journey" that Judy is alluding to began with Jan Christine Allard's entrance into the world in Edmonton on April 29, 1984. Jan—who quickly asserts that her name is not short for "Janet" or "Janice" or anything else, "just Jan!"—was the second-born child for Judy and Jim, joining big brother Jason. The family's common initials suggest a powerfully supportive bond, one that is expressed in the way that Judy continually coaches Jan, the affectionate humour with which Jim speaks of his daughter and in the enthusiastic appreciativeness of Jan's own tone when she speaks of her much-loved older sibling, Jason ("He's awesome!").

Mutual support and strength have characterized the Allards' response to the challenges posed by the special needs of their youngest child, who was diagnosed with Mosaic Down syndrome shortly after her birth. Jan has required special educational and support services throughout her life, and will continue to require assistance and monitoring as she now makes the transition to a more independent life as an adult woman. With the tremendous support and encouragement of her family, she has truly blossomed, more often than not outstripping the expectations placed upon her by professional assessment measures and scores. As Judy Allard, herself a teacher, observes, "All through the years, we always heard—and I always *knew*—that she had so much more ability than what she would sometimes show, or people would think she would have, because she had quite a speech delay when she was younger. But the ability was always much higher than what [tests] actually showed."

Jan's ability is such that she has not only completed her high school education in St. Albert through an integrated Independent Living Program, but has recently made a significant stride onwards to post-secondary training. Today, she is an extremely productive and socially engaged member of various communities: educational, civic, spiritual, and athletic. In the past, Jan has given back to the school system that nurtured her by working as a teacher's assistant and an office clerk at both the local Catholic high school and the school district office. She loves the ordered and structured environment of business offices, and aspires to work in such a setting full-time someday. Jan currently assists with clerical duties at SAIF, a St. Albert organization working to end family violence. As a resident of St. Albert, Jan has also volunteered her time planting flowers for the City, and worked as a volunteer at the Northern Alberta Children's Festival—both in the arts and crafts tent, and as member of the "Green Team" recycling crew. At her church, she has been an altar server, greeter, and a member of the youth group.

The extensive scope and generosity of Jan's volunteer commitments and achievements are astonishing for someone of her age. Yet she also manages to find time in her schedule for favorite interests and activities that are just what one might expect of a young 20-something. Fascinated with pop culture, she is an avid reader of celebrity magazines, an interest she supplements by watching her favorite television shows and occasionally checking out Sony's entertainment site on the web. (Ask her anything about celebrities like Rosie O'Donnell or the acting twins, Mary Kate and Ashley Olsen, and she will know the answer!) Jan also likes hanging out at malls, going bowling and heading out to Bud's Lounge in St. Albert to belt out a few karaoke songs. Jan and her friends, including her current boyfriend Josh, are also ardent hockey fans. On any Edmonton Oilers' game night, chances are you'll find her gathered somewhere with friends, maybe indulging in her favorite meal of pepperoni pizza (especially if the pie comes from Pizza Hut). In fact, that is exactly what Jan has planned on the Sunday afternoon I first meet her. By the end of our interview, I can tell that she is anxious to stop talking about herself and get to her hockey party.

But make no mistake: Jan is no armchair athlete. She has the ribbons from several Special Olympics competitions and the 2005 St. Albert Athlete of the Year Award to prove it. Floor hockey and swimming are especially favoured pursuits, but Jan has also participated in track and field and played soccer and baseball. She has tried everything from pilates to kickboxing to "cardioblast" work outs. As Jim Allard notes, she also takes great pleasure riding the bike trails in and around St. Albert with him and Judy. (Jan owns a specially equipped adult tricycle.) When the Allards visit relatives in Nova Scotia, Jan has a blast riding quads and fishing near her grandpa's cabin in Kenziville. And, of course, diving in the ocean with cousins Sarah and Ruth along for company.

Given Jan's love of music and singing, it is hardly surprising that her physical activities have long extended into the sphere of dance as well. From the time she was a young child, Jan has enjoyed a variety of tap, jazz and ballet classes, even performing in local festivals with St. Albert's Dance Company. As for that basketball hoop outside the family home, that's the legacy of brother Jason, who is now studying International Business and no longer lives at home. For Jan, who is barely five feet tall, basketball may be the one activity that remains a bit of a stretch.

Curled up in an over-sized sofa chair, and casually dressed in black sweats, Jan has the natural look that goes with her active lifestyle. Though her sparkling strawberry blonde hair is fashionably streaked with highlights, the rosy hue of her complexion is all her own. Each time we meet, she wears neither make-up nor jewelry. In many ways, she is a shorter and rounder version of her mother, a stylish blonde woman who is also active in fitness and sports. The two women are a study in complementary contrasts in ways that go beyond appearances, too.

"I'm quiet," Jan admits, still curled in the big sofa chair.

"And I talk a lot," Judy confesses.

They are speaking of the morning hours, specifically. As opposed to her mother's "morning lark" habits, Jan is a natural "night owl." Consequently, when Jan gets absorbed by a good movie or book at night, she isn't always—as Judy suggests with a laugh—thrilled by injunctions to "put the light out" or "stop reading!" Nevertheless, each weekday, Jan sets her alarm clock for 6:30 a.m. By 7:16, she's out the door and into the early morning winter darkness, ready to board the first of two buses that will shuttle her down the St. Albert Trail to the busy northern district of Edmonton's downtown, where she now attends college.

This morning routine is a major achievement, for despite Jan's love of structured order, one of the intriguing paradoxes of her character is that she is free from conventional senses of the relevance or importance of clock time, a fact perhaps related to her problems with short-term memory.

"Time doesn't mean anything to her," Jim says, emphatically. "She's a slow mover."

"*Some*times." Judy interjects.

"You tell her, 'hurry up, we gotta go'—we're in a big rush, and she'll take her own time. She gets in that bathroom..." Jim trails off momentarily. "A typical woman," he sighs.

A constant stream of traffic flows along Princess Elizabeth Avenue, the major thoroughfare leading to the Northern Alberta Institute of Technology (NAIT). Sharp little Cessna cargo planes needle in for high-pitched landings at the nearby municipal airport; larger, dull-colored military craft drone in and out. On campus, students pour between buildings, milling at entrances for impromptu conferences and quick smokes, hailing one another with shouts of "how's it goin' crew?" Even with an enrollment of several thousand students, the school maintains an intimate atmosphere. Many students and faculty seem to recognize each another. However, its main campus in the Edmonton Capital region is easily big enough to get lost in—as I discover one frigid winter morning when I arrive to meet Jan for a personal tour of her school. It is -15° Celsius, but colder than that with a mean wind chill and light flurries. By the time I find my way from the visitor's parking lot to the coffee shop where I am to meet Jan and her program facilitator, Pamela Johnson, my gloved fingers are numb and I am quite late.

Jan and Pam are patiently sipping almost-finished hot chocolates when I rush by, initially missing them at their table. "That's her," Jan will quietly report to Pam, who is the one to call out after me. Jan greets me with a shy smile as I sit down. She is wearing a delicate pink wool cardigan and matching top that sets off her complexion and smoky blue eyes. Although she looks composed, Jan is not feeling well today, Pam tells me. But Jan insists that she is still well enough to escort me around the NAIT campus, where she is currently enrolled in the Office and Records Program, taking courses such as document processing and keyboarding. Jan is progressing very well in her studies, reinforcing once again her family's confidence and pride in her sometimes hidden, but real, ability levels.

Bidding farewell to Pam, Jan navigates our way expertly down long corridors, past rooms full of glass tubing, mechanical pumps, and people wearing industrial safety glasses. She leads me to the classroom wing where she takes keyboarding. The long banks of black and silent monitors look a little intimidating, but Jan isn't afraid of computers, and she clearly loves her keyboarding class, shyly pointing to the work station near the front of the room where she prefers to sit.

Every Wednesday, after exercising her fingers and mind in class, Jan gives the rest of herself a good work out: namely, in the hip hop aerobics class that she takes on campus. Past the huge school gymnasium, up a flight of stairs, we peer into a beautifully lit, quiet studio with hardwood floors. Jan beams when she looks into this sanctuary. She has always enjoyed the expressive arts of dance, music, and singing, so a hip hop dance class seems like a natural choice for her to unwind and relax after classes.

But neither the hip hop studio, nor the student pub—where Jan meets with friends on the occasional Friday—seem likely choices today. By the time we get to her locker, and she slings a thick backpack of traveling things over her shoulder, her cold seems to be worsening, and I am getting anxious to see her to her bus. Even so, she remains an ever-gracious host, at one point pausing at the top of a narrow set of stairs to usher me ahead with a small flourish of her arm.

At the bus bay, her cough has worsened, and her eyes and nose have started to run. I dig around in my purse for some cough drops. What seems remarkable though, is that the more miserable Jan is clearly starting to feel, the more talkative she becomes, her earlier reserve evaporating entirely as we sit inside, waiting for the number 202 bus. She chats to me about her brother, Jason, about how she sometimes likes to browse through a copy of the NAIT student newspaper *The Nugget* and about the headaches she sometimes suffers, pounding one fist into the other open palm to reinforce the point of their severity. She doesn't seem concerned about missing her bus, which I keep scanning for, nervously recalling her parents' gentle ribbing that "time doesn't mean anything to her." On the other hand, she has never had a problem getting herself to and from school; a few transit drivers, she notes, will greet her as a regular. With her bus due to arrive, she blows her nose, zips up her blue parka and pulls on some matching mittens. I watch her start to make her way, coughing, through the snow flurries. I am thinking about the courage it must take for her to venture out into the world alone. But she is thinking of something else. Before she crosses the street, she stops, turns around, and croaks out a polite thanks for the cough drops. They don't seem to be helping, but this is Jan. The girl who made the 'Welcome' sign adorning her family home apparently never forgets her manners.

Judy and I are sitting in the Allard's dining room, sipping tea and poring over a table covered in Jan's drawings, paintings, and sketches, when a loud crash sounds directly above our heads, shaking the chandelier slightly.

"Oh, that's just Jan, jumping off her bed," Judy explains, without a missing a beat. "She jumps off her bed to help her reach things high up on her bookshelf. One of these days, she's going to come right through that ceiling."

Moments later, Jan comes bounding back into the room with the prized photograph that had been beyond her reach. She has recovered fully from the serious case of strep throat that had been coming on when I last saw her. The photograph she proudly shows me is a head shot of her with her boyfriend, Josh. They are leaning into one another, smiling broadly. The Allard home is full of family photos—on the mantle in the family room and filling glass display shelves in the comfortably appointed front sitting room. There is even an album of photos from Jan's recent Christmas Disney World cruise with Judy and Jim. In one snapshot, Jan is dressed up for dinner, and elegantly made up, with lipstick and eye shadow. She looks every inch the pretty adult woman she is, except that she is also posing with Mickey Mouse, and the expression of glee on her face is wholly unrestrained.

But it is Jan's own artwork that I've come to take a look at today, and eventually we turn back to the sketch books, albums, notebooks and loose leaf works piled up on the table before us. These are creative works that Jan has produced over many years. There are pictures of animals—whales jumping from water, horses rearing, kittens curled up, a cow munching on a flower. There are pictures of geometric shapes and houses and buildings, including a couple of the office tower buildings which are on Jan's mind nowadays, as she begins to pursue her adult career goals. Perhaps most remarkable are Jan's images of people. Her portraits of faces are rendered in a distinctive, consistent style that is minimalist, but incredibly expressive. Almost all the faces sport thick page-boy hair cuts that frame the face like inverted U's, noses that resemble upside-down 7's, and eyes that glance off awry—a sideways gaze that imparts to Jan's portraits an irresistibly mischievous effect. My favorite is her picture of "Rosie," a lone female figure, who stands out in the foreground of a gently sloping, green grass landscape, one single tree off to the side. The figure has long legs that look like a nutcracker—solid and strong. Her torso consists of a red triangle with an emblazoned inscription that announces her name as "Rosie." Rosie's face is framed by a wonderful shock of electric blue hair, the thick texture of which matches the consistency of the single tree's greenery, off to the side. The picture is beautifully vivid in its colours, joyous in its vision.

Before my visit ends, Judy and I find ourselves encouraging Jan to get back to her artwork. Though her schedule is tight these days, with her studies at NAIT, her volunteer work, her social life and sporting events, visual art is clearly another realm in which she has aptitude and further potential. Unlike her sideways-glancing portrait people, Jan fixes me with a clear, unblinking, steady gaze when we say goodbye. She is a woman who is looking forward in all senses, and with good reason. Even this very day, Jan is once again looking ahead with happy anticipation. It's Valentine's Day, and she has a dinner date lined up with Josh.

by
Dan RUBINSTEIN

A Special Kind of Love

Goodsoil, Saskatchewan is a quintessential prairie outpost. The name is perfect. So is the population: 284, according to the 2001 census— and that count has never changed much, says the cheery woman who answers phones at the village office. Founded as the St. Boniface Colony by German-Catholic settlers from southwestern Saskatchewan in the 1920s, Goodsoil and the adjacent fertile lands held promises of the good life for people willing to work hard and pray harder.

The village's defining features today mirror those of small communities throughout the west. It has wilderness: located seventy kilometres east of Cold Lake, Alberta, Goodsoil is the gateway to Meadow Lake Provincial Park. It has history: a cairn outside the museum marks the spot where the Cree released their prisoners after the 1885 Riel Rebellion. It has an oversized landmark: twenty-foot-tall Goodsoil Gus, an axe-toting wooden lumberjack who watches over the tourist information centre. And, naturally, it has produced a hockey star: Ron Greschner, who spent his entire seventeen-season NHL career with the New York Rangers.

April 16, 1983 was a typical day in Goodsoil. A wedding day. Sepia-toned photographs in a binder with "Our Wedding" embossed on the cover tell the tale of Karen Gurski and Clement Lefebvre's nuptials. The groom, with his bushy eighties hair and moustache, decorates his equally-mustached and bushy-haired brother-in-law's Camero with white and yellow paper carnations. The bride, cradling a bouquet of real flowers, grins bashfully as her mother affixes a veil to her white gown. Karen sits between her parents in dad's boat-sized green Oldsmobile for the drive to church. Karen and Clem bow their heads as longtime Gurski family priest Father Ron reads from the bible.

"My knees were shaking like crazy," says Clem, hovering over the photo album.

"We were both pretty nervous," Karen giggles.

Keep flipping pages and you see more than the formal ceremony. There's the reception in the Goodsoil hall; village ladies cooked up a feast for the nearly 300 guests. There's Karen's brother, Ken, who took a public speaking course, stubby beer bottle in hand, working the crowd as the master of ceremonies. And there's Clem, on one knee, removing Karen's garter while she daintily balances on one foot, on display in front of so many relatives and friends.

"You turned so red," Karen says, giving her husband of twenty-three years, the father of their two children, a playful poke.

Clem is turning red now.

Even though his marriage to Karen made the papers, Clem is not accustomed to this sort of attention. The *Edmonton Sun* wrote about Karen and Clem getting engaged. The headline, "A Special Kind Of Love," could be from any era, although the header above it, "Retarded Couple Plans To Marry," uses jarringly antiquated language. The article explains that Karen and Clem "suffer from mild degrees of mental retardation." Nowadays we don't say "suffer," and the stark term "retardation" has been replaced by "developmental" or "intellectual" disability.

Despite its flaws, the article is precious to Clem's older sister, Vivian Gazelle. She unfolds the yellowed newspaper clipping and fills in the blanks when a stranger peppers Karen and Clem with questions about the minutiae of their wedding. This is fine with Clem. He and Vivian, the two youngest children in a family with eleven kids, are beyond close. Vivian was the angel who, in Clem's words, "pulled" the despondent twenty-year-old from his hometown, Cold Lake, to Edmonton. Which is the reason he met Karen, who was similarly "pulled" to Edmonton by her brother, Ken. Which is the reason their love took root.

Clement Lefebvre was born in Cold Lake in 1957. Some of his childhood memories are good, he says. But mostly he remembers endless chores on the family farm. Like milking cows. "We milked by hand," he says. "We milked a lot of cows." Clem did go fishing—but he's not talking about lazy afternoons at the lake. Dad would drill two holes in the ice and drop a net into the frigid waters (it was Cold Lake, after all). The kids had to do the grunt work to snare enough fish for the family.

"Everything we did was more or less for our subsistence," says Vivian.

"I didn't do many fun things," adds Clem, his confidence—and memory—seemingly sparked by Vivian's readiness to share stories. "It was all work, work, work."

"That," says Vivian, "was our childhood."

Yet they laugh at many of the memories, time and distance supplanting pain with humour. They're laughing now. "Remember…" Clem says to Vivian, barely able to get the words out through his chuckling, "remember when I set the baseball diamond on fire?"

"Everybody in town," says Vivian, "knows *this* story."

"I had found a pack of matches," Clem explains. "I just wanted to see what they would do…But I helped put out the fire, too! We didn't have to call the fire department. The whole neighbourhood came with gunny sacks full of water."

Clem stops laughing when asked about school. It was three blocks from home, and he failed several grades. Whenever Vivian stepped into the hallway for lunch or recess, Clem was usually there already, kicked out of class. With no extra help from his teachers, he barely reached grade eight. Then it was down to Edmonton to live with Vivian and attend "special classes" at high school. He lived on his own in grade twelve, in a basement apartment. But after graduation, it was back to Cold Lake to work on the farm. For six years. And that's when Clem hit bottom.

"After the chores and all the work was done," he says, "there was nothing else to do. I'd go to the corner store, just walk around." Until Clem wrote Vivian a fateful letter. "He sounded like he was very depressed," she recalls. "He was bored with life and didn't care about anything." So in 1980, she pulled him to the city for good.

Clem started working for the painting and construction company owned by Vivian's husband, Chris Gazelle. Painting can be dangerous, however, and Clem made mistakes that sound positively slapstick were they not so serious. Like the time he swung around while holding a piece of lumber and nearly knocked a co-worker off a set of scaffolding. Or when—because Clem had been told to drop everything when somebody yelled "coffee break"—he reacted literally and stopped holding the ladder Chris was atop (painting Peter Pocklington's house, no less). The ladder began to topple and Clem had to recover fast to prevent his brother-in-law from tumbling two stories.

Clem and Vivian are laughing again. "I was glad to come to Edmonton," he says, pointing a finger at Vivian, "but many times you said you'd send me back."

After two weeks of painting, Vivian helped Clem fill out an application for training and work at Goodwill Industries. After registering, as required, for Alberta's Assured Income for the Severely Handicapped or AISH program, he started stuffing envelopes and moving boxes in a warehouse. He hasn't injured anybody on the job since.

There are echoes of Clem's story in Karen Gurski's childhood. Born in a Regina hospital in 1958, she grew up in Goodsoil, fed chickens and fetched eggs on the family farm, yelled for dad when bears wandered into town, swam in the lake and had tea parties with friends, and has hazy memories of her grandparents getting kidnapped and rescued, tied up, in a chicken coop. With no extra help at school, she struggled as far as grade eight. Then she dropped out and got paid work, cleaning cabins and doing janitorial chores at the village co-op and bank.

In 1979, Karen's brother Ken—who is now a social worker—encouraged her to move to Edmonton. There was nothing for her in Goodsoil, he knew, and she didn't mind the city. "It's nice to meet different people," says Karen, "and do different things."

Karen also landed at Goodwill Industries. Although she eventually waitressed and worked at a couple of daycares through Goodwill, she started in the workshop and graduated to the cafeteria, where she learned how to cook. And every morning at ten o'clock, Clem walked in for his break.

At the time, Clem was already dating another woman named Karen. But when he saw the second Karen sitting in a booth by herself, he sat down and said hello. "He saw me first," says Karen. "I didn't know who he was at all."

The first Karen was a smoker, which Clem never liked. And when she started a fire in the Goodwill washroom, she was sent to the Alberta

Hospital for psychiatric care. Clem visited her there until he met the new Karen. Their first date was a movie at the old Paramount Theatre on Jasper Avenue. They watched a lot of James Bond films together. They went bowling. They joked about how Karen number two framed Karen number one by setting that bathroom fire. Karen says she doesn't remember their first kiss. Clem says "oh yeah" when asked about it.

After dating for about a year, they moved in together. Then Clem bought a ring, and over dinner at the Old Spaghetti Factory, he said, "I guess we might as well get married."

"My mom didn't like Clem at first," says Karen. "But she got used to him."

Clem's family was more divided. "I heard people say, 'How can he get married, with his disabilities?'" says Vivian. They wondered how the couple would function and support themselves on their own. "I heard that kind of talk. It always came down to his disabilities. They just couldn't see him getting married. But despite everything that everybody said, nobody was going to stop them."

The phone rings in Clem and Karen's small west Edmonton bungalow. They bought the house, their first, in 2005 when Clem inherited some money after his mother died. It's their son Sean on the line. He's just a few months shy of his seventeenth birthday. Today he's buying his first car. Because he is the only family member without a disability and with a driver's license, Sean will become their designated driver.

Clem and Karen wrestle with the same anxieties as all parents. They worry about their twenty-year-old daughter Jennifer, who has a learning disability. She completed the Integrated Opportunities program at St. Joseph's High School (the type of program that didn't exist when Karen and Clem were students) and works as a gas station cashier. Karen thinks it's dangerous for Jenn to work at night. Customers swear at her because of high gas prices, because the pumps are slow, because she dares insist they butt out their cigarettes while filling up. Customers yell and she has to bite her tongue and smile—and she's not one for that.

Clem takes Jenn's grad picture and one of Sean's hockey photos off the bookshelf. They're both at work now, so these photos will have to serve as stand-ins for the proud parents. Karen tells Jennifer's birth story. She was born at six o'clock in the morning, after seventeen hours of labour. "It wasn't fun," says Karen. "I didn't have an epidural."

"I put my hands in the air," says Clem. "I didn't know what to do."

Nor did some of his siblings. "Everybody was shocked," says Vivian. "People wondered how they'd do with kids. Because at this point they were on their own. I wasn't involved in their lives much. I had kids of my own and we were running a business."

Although a nurse's aide helped the couple with newborn Jennifer, teaching diapering and feeding skills, those early days were demanding. The baby cried often; she had eye surgery. And three years later, she was jealous when Sean was born.

Six days after Sean buys his first car, a 1998 Sunfire, it's already dented. He was backing out of a friend's driveway and bumped something. But the dent is "barely noticeable," he protests. Aunt Vivian jokes that the stranger in the living room is an insurance inspector. Sean's parents grin, and his sister punctuates her laughter with a gleeful clap. Despite their hectic schedules, Sean and Jenn have cleared a couple of hours to talk.

Sean works at the West Edmonton Mall water park. His post is at the bottom of the waterslide. If people are drowning, he jumps in and saves them. A grade eleven student, Sean enjoys his industrial arts classes and is thinking about getting his welding ticket. "I like working with my hands," he says. "I don't think I could stand a desk job."

Sean is a typical teenaged boy. He has shoulder-length hair and fidgets with any object within reach. He plays video games and shoots hoops with friends. At home, programming the VCR and telephone voicemail is his responsibility. Sean is more mature than your average 16-year-old. Even when his father teases him about the hair—"Sean, for your graduation, that mop is gonna be cut"—he succinctly explains that he shaved his head a year ago for a cancer fundraiser and has simply been "too lazy" to go to the barber.

Sometimes, Sean admits, mom and dad embarrass him. But only because they're his parents and he's a teenager. He doesn't remember ever being hassled about Karen and Clem by classmates. ("Only by me," quips Jenn.) Sean does acknowledge that growing up with parents and a sister who have disabilities has affected his life. "I've got a grip on things," says

Sean. "Sometimes I really have to be serious. In stressful situations, I've had to be the authority figure in the house."

Sean stopped Jenn the first time she tried to cut herself with a steak knife. It happened two years ago, when Jenn was eighteen. A nasty breakup triggered feelings she had been battling for years. "The best way I can describe it," she says though tears, accepting a box of tissue from her mother, "is like opening a can of pop that's been shaken."

The second time Sean wasn't there. Jenn rolls up both sleeves to show the self-inflicted scars. A school counselor saw the fresh wounds and drove Jenn to the hospital. She was put on seventy-two-hour lockdown in a windowless psych-ward room. "They asked me all the usual questions," says Jenn. "It felt like jail." She was deemed high-risk for suicide.

When the school phoned Karen, she called Vivian immediately. Vivian rushed to the hospital; Karen, Clem and Sean followed. Which is why, when Jenn is asked how she found her way whole again, she gives an instant one-word answer. It's the same answer as the one given by Clem, when asked what saved him from despair in Cold Lake: *family*.

"I didn't go as far as cutting myself," says Clem. "But I was very depressed. I didn't know what I would do next."

Vivian rubs Jenn's back as she relives her own ordeal. She's been more than an aunt since Jenn lived with Vivian's family for a year. In grade eight, Jenn felt besieged—by classes, by bullies—at school. Her parents weren't coping well, either. Living on two AISH incomes and Clem's part-time jobs, such as delivering flyers, they couldn't manage their money. There was never much food at home. "We couldn't do it anymore," says Clem.

"But they didn't want to bother anybody," says Vivian, who nevertheless decided to get her own family profoundly involved—after their hiatus—in her brother's life. Edmonton Persons with Developmental Disabilities (PDD) provides funds for a support worker to come to their house once a week to help with chores such as shopping and budgeting. But most of the help these days comes from Vivian, Chris and their kids; they offer drives, for instance—anywhere, anytime.

"It's hard when you're a family and you see some people thriving while others are not doing well," says Vivian. "I wanted to share my family's luck—and I got more out of this experience than I thought possible. The biggest thing is that my kids have learned about sharing. They share their time, their money, everything."

Jenn has a star tattooed on the back of her neck. She calls it her guiding light. She rolls up a pant leg to reveal another tattoo: pink carnations bursting out of a vase. It's dedicated to her grandmother, Clem's mom. "It's forever," Jenn says poetically, before adding, "Well, you can laser it off, but that's like $5,000."

Vivian rolls her eyes. "At least you got it here," she says to Jenn. "My kids got theirs in Mexico."

Jenn is set to quit her gas station job. She'd rather work retail, maybe in a clothing store. She's also finishing two courses, by correspondence, to get her high school diploma; she has an Integrated Opportunities certificate for now. Jenn wants to study either massage therapy or music therapy next. The self-proclaimed "school band geek," who cried when her parents surprised her with a clarinet last Christmas, wants to explore how music can calm people with disabilities or help them with coordination and exercise. "Music has always been my special thing," she says. "There's a baby picture of me with headphones."

Jenn worked as a janitor at her high school to pay for her own braces, tattoos and a band trip to Vancouver. She is textbook-determined. Like her parents, she doesn't learn as quickly as most people. If she doesn't "get" a concept right away, it can be a fight to figure it out. "I've always had a learning disability," she says with look-you-in-the-eyes clarity, "but that's never stopped me from doing whatever I wanted. There's always going to be a label on me. But it doesn't matter."

Last June, the Lefebvres drove to Cold Lake in Sean's car. It was the first time the four travelled like this, alone and together. They go north often, to both Goodsoil and Cold Lake, to visit relatives. They ride on ATVs and pick Saskatoon berries. Last year, at Lac des Iles in Meadow Lake Provincial Park, they saw dozens of pelicans on a spit jutting out into the water.

"They just sat there," says Jenn.

"Chillin'," says Sean.

Jenn, Sean, Karen and Clem finish each other sentences. Disjointed memories meld into stories. The conversation jumps from strategies for their upcoming garage sale to Karen's sole soap-opera addiction (*Days of Our Lives*) to Clem's gardening exploits (he grows carrots, peas and kohlrabi but has trouble identifying weeds). That segues into a debate over the definitions of techno and "emo" music, which somehow segues into a thread about Clem's many nicknames, such as Clem Chowder and Clem Kadiddlehopper, the country bumpkin character on Red Skelton's television and radio shows.

"But you know," Vivian says to her brother, "you could have been called worse."

A horn beeps outside the house and Jenn leaps up from the couch. Her ride to a party is here. "Don't judge a book by its cover," she advises when asked for some parting wisdom. "And never say never."

"I don't see myself with a disability," Clem says when Jenn is out the door. "I just do whatever I have to do to support my family. It's as simple as that. And if I had to do it all over again, I would."

"Clem and his family have taught me more about life than I could have ever dreamed," says Vivian. "It's about being who you are."

She's talking directly to Clem now.

"You never really pretended," she says. "You're just Clem."

by
Michelle PONICH

Big Enough Dreams

The petite brunette woman stood in the hotel elevator, dwarfed by the broad, square body of opera legend Luciano Pavarotti. He rested one hand on her shoulder, while he stroked her face with the other and whispered "Bella, Bella." Tanya Ponich had been imagining this moment for a long time. Pavarotti's music had been part of her life from the day she had taken her first breath. Now the great tenor was inviting her to have her picture taken with him.

For many people, meeting Pavarotti would be an exciting and memorable occasion. But for my mother Rosalind and I, standing just outside that crowded elevator, the encounter between my sister and Pavarotti held an even deeper meaning. We were witnessing the fulfillment of a lifelong dream by someone who had never been expected to live long enough to have any dreams at all.

When my sister Tanya was born in 1979, our mother was told that not only did her new baby have Down's syndrome, but also leukemia. Tanya's white cell count was extremely low and she was running a high fever. She was not expected to live for more than a month. Mom didn't accept that verdict—her mother's intuition wouldn't allow her. "From the time she was born there was something within her personality. She had this little fight, this little drive, she never ever gave up," Mom says. A few days later, Tanya's fever broke and her white cell count had risen. It turned out that Mom was right, she didn't have leukemia at all.

Before leaving the hospital, Mom made a deal with her new baby. As she wrapped Tanya in a blanket, she looked into her eyes and whispered "I'll try if you will; we're in this together." Try is what Tanya has done. Starting with her earliest year, the expectations placed on her were no different than the ones that were placed on me. Mom decided that Tanya would read, write, and be more than just "socially acceptable." She was determined that both her daughters would be taught to be polite, compassionate, and respectful.

When our mother brought Tanya home after her bumpy first days in the hospital, she wanted to find a way to soothe her new baby. As she put Tanya to bed on her first night at home, Mom played a tape of Pavarotti. Over the years this became a bedtime ritual, to the point that Tanya learned many of the Italian classics and would sing along with recordings of the great opera singer.

Tanya's education began early. By the time she was three years old, she was being picked up by Barrel Taxi every morning and driven to the early childhood intervention program at Mayfield Elementary School. Tanya also became the subject of research studies and the focus of a young woman's thesis for the University of Alberta.

Tanya was four when our family moved to Victoria. This presented a challenge for her and for our parents, because Victoria had fewer resources and programs for children with developmental disabilities than did Edmonton. Mom discovered a Montessori school and met with two of its teachers. They were keen but apprehensive at the prospect of having a student with Down syndrome. Mom suggested that they accept Tanya for a month. If it wasn't working by then, she would take Tanya out of the school. That day never came. The hands-on environment and small class sizes allowed Tanya to learn and grow at a pace that worked for her.

Tanya's integration into a regular classroom lasted right through her schooling, with the exception of her first year of high school. Tanya was to attend the secondary school that I attended. It had a special education program and Mom felt that this might be the best way to help Tanya make the transition into a new setting. Unfortunately, we soon discovered that she was not thriving. Tanya is well mannered and was uncomfortable with the poor behavior of many of the students in the special education program. By the end of the first year, Mom knew that Tanya was not going to grow if she continued in that program. She went to the principal and asked if they could try something different. If Tanya was accompanied by an aide, could she be integrated into a regular classroom? The principal was willing to make the attempt. Tanya's high school experience improved after that. She made a lifelong friend with a young woman named Laila. Tanya joined the school choir and toured California and Hawaii with them. In the end, she not only had a somewhat 'typical' high school learning experience but a positive social life as well.

Today, Tanya pushes herself constantly whether at work or play. She realizes that she has to work harder at life because she has Down's syndrome. One of her greatest frustrations is not being able to achieve the things she wants as soon as she wants. Tanya has big dreams. Her commitments and passions sometimes border on obsessions but this is how she is able to get things done.

One of Tanya's current big dreams is that of being a writer for her favorite television soap opera, *Days of Our Lives*. It all began a few years ago. Tanya had been watching the show regularly and felt that the story line was not going the way she thought it should. Tanya wrote to the producers over and over, without reply. Then she decided to take action.

"If I become a writer on *Days* then I can change the story line," she said. Tanya faithfully watched and taped the show everyday. She began to rewrite episodes that she didn't like. One day it dawned on her that she would have to move to Hollywood to work on the show. This idea didn't bother her at all. It did cause some concern for our mother, however. She finally told Tanya that she couldn't move to Hollywood.

"I had to get her to stop," says Mom. "She needed to realize the reality of the situation and how hard it actually was to achieve this dream of hers." Mom told Tanya that no one could just arrive in Hollywood and be hired as a writer for a major television series. Writers usually go to school to develop effective writing skills. Even this information didn't deter Tanya. A few months later, she enrolled in a script writing course at Edmonton's MacEwan College.

Since taking the course, Tanya has written and produced a twenty-minute soap opera. Jordan, a summer intern at SKILLS Society in Edmonton, was able to find the actors and camera operator to help bring the script to life. Tanya's friend Bonnie assisted Tanya in crafting her script and coming up with the characters' names. Going through every stage of the production process, Tanya learned what it took to create and produce a soap opera. Tanya still wants to hold a public screening but is waiting until Jordan returns to Edmonton. She now realizes that writing is hard work, but is stilling chasing that dream. If anything, the dream has grown—now Tanya wants to own her own production studio and to produce a soap opera without commercials.

Not everything has gone so smoothly for Tanya. A year ago, she underwent a life-altering experience—the loss of a parent. During most of our growing up years, our father suffered from Parkinson's disease. In 2005 he lost his battle with that illness. As a family we decided that Tanya was not going to be sheltered or protected from what was happening; she had to be allowed to experience and grieve his loss, just like everyone else in the family. And although she was sad, confused, and scared, Tanya decided she wanted to speak at the memorial service.

Most people would have difficulty speaking at the funeral of a parent. As Tanya stood at the podium, she was shaking. Then she took a deep breath, lifted her head high, and spoke from her heart. "Dad, I didn't want you to die," she began. She continued to speak about Dad and his illness. She closed her speech by saying that our dad had gone to heaven to be with our grandparents. "One day," she said, "I'll be there too."

Tanya was dignified and composed as she walked slowly back to her seat, next to our cousin Scott. As he put his arm around her shoulders, Tanya began to cry. Her sobs were so natural and real, that for once in her life her label—developmentally disabled—was invisible.

A year later, Tanya still feels the loss of our father. She has a deep faith in God and often turns to the church for comfort. John Privett, the minister at Christ Church—the congregation to which Tanya belongs—has become one of her closest confidantes. Tanya books regular "coffee times" with John. Together they explore her questions about life and death. "What does heaven look like?" Tanya asks. "What does my dad want from me now that he is gone?"

John does his best to answer Tanya's questions and give her a sense of peace. He also gains much from his meetings with Tanya. "She really forces me to think about the questions I have," he says.

John isn't the only person who has benefited from knowing Tanya. For the past eight years, Tanya has been spending two days a week at the gym with her trainer Janey. Before Janey started training Tanya, she described her own approach to training as "systematic and technical, fairly methodical with progression." After working with Tanya, Janey "had to abandon that completely." She had to become more flexible and think differently. In doing so, new opportunities and possibilities arose. "Tanya is a great life coach," says Janey. "She has taught me to be a little sillier and perhaps walk with a bit of a lighter foot."

At the age of twenty-seven, Tanya has blossomed into her own person. She gives back to her community by volunteering at three different Edmonton locations two days each week. Tanya has been a long time volunteer at the General Hospital, helping with office work at the Centre for Lung Health and on 8Y, the floor where our dad lived during his illness. Hardisty Recreation Centre has also opened its doors to Tanya, not only as a patron, but as a 'facility assistant.' She is in charge of designing and creating exhibits for the display case. During the past year, Tanya has also been working at the office at Christ Church one morning each week. She helps assemble the worship bulletin and has tea and cookies with the ladies in the office.

Tanya recognizes the value of getting up every day and going out the door and doing something. While some people may view the work that she does as boring or menial, Tanya is able to walk in the door, talk to the other staff and do her job with a sense of purpose.

As for Tanya's future, her dreams continue to be as big and as hopeful as those of any other woman the same age. She wants to live on her own and have a boyfriend who is kind, loving, and good-looking. Most of all, Tanya wants to achieve things with her life. I believe she will be able to do just that.

Part of my belief is rooted in my experience with Tanya on that spring night a few years ago. Mom, Tanya, and I had come to Calgary to see Pavarotti in concert. Throughout the evening, Tanya insisted that we would meet Pavarotti in person. We tried to convince her that this was highly unlikely, but without success. After the concert we found ourselves back at our hotel. After a bite to eat we wandered into the lobby. I turned around just as Pavarotti entered the hotel. As he strode over to the elevator, security guard in tow, I looked at Tanya and said, "follow him." She moved swiftly but the elevator door closed in her face. Mom punched the "up" button and the doors opened. Tanya looked at Pavarotti and Mom blurted out to the security guard "can I speak to him?" Pavarotti looked at us and said "Si." Tanya stepped into the elevator and for a few short, wonderful minutes, she and her greatest hero created a priceless memory.

As she stood in that elevator, Tanya proved to me once again that almost anything is possible if your dream is big enough.

by
Lorie MISECK and Beverly MacKINNON

The Blue Folder

"*My eyes open to let the world in.*"

(*from "*Curtain," *a poem by Beverly MacKinnon*)

———————

For the past month I've had in my possession a blue folder that's colour is so intense it has stung against the palette of the grey shadows and perennial white of yet another slow ending to an Edmonton winter. The folder and its contents belong to Beverly MacKinnon. Thick with photocopies of awards and certificates; with stories and poems she has written; with newspaper articles and letters of reference and backgrounders on her life. If this folder was found by a stranger, its contents would tell Beverly's unique personal story.

I met Beverly for the first time on an unseasonably warm and sunny February afternoon at her home in south Edmonton. I entered a house saturated in sunlight and passed by a wall of what appeared to be an endless green hum of plants of various shapes, sizes and growing regions thriving against a large living room window. From small succulents to broader fleshy plants, they leaned into the sunlight.

What struck me upon meeting Beverly were her eyes. They were alive, clear and direct, also lit with an intensity that comes from clarity and conviction. We had coffee and talked for two hours. On the drive home I thought about the conversation we had and her openness about her life. I had left her house inspired, but also feeling a tinge of shame.

When I am at my best, I believe there are no accidents. I was finishing an essay about how I hated reading as a child, when I got the call to write a profile of Beverly—a woman who had struggled with literacy all her life. My shame came not from this contrast, but from my own struggle as a writer. I was wallowing in the shallow waters of self-pity (with a very small and insufficient flotation device) when I met this woman, who through her work and her attitude, taught me more about hope and community than I have learned in a while.

When I am at my best, I also believe that every person we meet has something to teach us beyond what is apparent and visible. In describing the commitment she made in her early thirties to learn to read, Beverly also taught me about passion and language and how we make choices. How one person can sit and wait to be invited to participate fully in life, while another can step far beyond what is deemed comfortable and safe, in order to learn.

I'm not sure if anyone reading this, myself included, can fully appreciate the implications of being illiterate. Go without reading for one day—anything, anywhere. Then, when you choose not to read, recognize it as a choice, rather than being unable to read. Think of how you might be able to find your way to work on a bus, understand the labels on foods or medicine, or if you have children, help them to navigate through their lives.

For most of us, reading is second nature, as automatic as breathing. This act is an act taken for granted. Yet about twenty-two percent of Canadian adults have serious problems dealing with printed material. According to World Literacy of Canada, Canadians with the lowest level of literacy skills have an unemployment rate of twenty-six percent compared to four percent for Canadians with the highest literacy levels. Nearly 1.4 million Canadian children fifteen years of age and younger are living in low-income homes, thirty-four percent of children from the lowest income families do not complete their high school education.

Beverly MacKinnon was one of those Canadians who passed through the public school system without ever learning to read more than a few words. Until grade ten she languished in what was called the "Opportunity Class." Beverly could understand concepts but could not read the material put in front of her. She remembers getting help from a friend who would read homework questions to her.

After leaving school, Beverly took cleaning jobs, working for the Royal Glenora Club, hospitals, and apartment buildings. An automobile accident slowed her down and gave her time to reflect on what she was doing with her life. She was in her early thirties and still reading at a grade two level. It was at that point that she decided that she was going to learn to read, no matter what the cost.

Last summer, roughly ten years after Beverly made that decision, she received the 2005 Canada Post Literacy Awards for Individual Achievement for the Province of Alberta. For the award ceremony, Canada Post flew her sister out from Ontario to celebrate. "I think my sister was really proud of me and my grandparents would have been really happy. Having my sister here was like having my grandparents here." The award also included the prize of a computer.

Since she first began her journey to overcome illiteracy, Beverly has been active in P.A.L.S. (Project Adult Literacy Society) and Prospects Literacy Society. She has taken a math class, a public speaking course, has appeared on radio and television and has written several children's stories and a few poems. She has volunteered in her daughter's school, eventually becoming the Volunteer Coordinator.

Beverly is also an active member of Students for Students Steering Committee at P.A.L.S. and sits on the board for Student Voices for Students. Students from various literacy organizations comprise the group. They meet to build confidence, self-esteem and are there for each other as general support. The group has presented to the University of Alberta and many public schools, at International Literacy Day and the John Howard Society, to name but a few. As a group they have written a list—part manifesto—of what having a voice means to them. "Having a voice is getting the word out, out for ourselves and others, telling our stories, telling what we went through, telling our accomplishments, sharing our thoughts." The final sentence on the list is "Having a voice is the power to change our lives."

After years of being unable to read, she learned. Why? She credits not only her accident, but the birth of her daughter Sarah. "Just because I couldn't read, I didn't want anyone to think I couldn't do my job as a mother," said Beverly. She said it hurt when she heard that her daughter told her teacher not to send anything home that had to be read, because her mother couldn't read. When her daughter was diagnosed as having learning disabilities as well as Attention Deficit Disorder (ADD), Beverly realized that she needed to learn. "If I couldn't help myself, then how could I help her?"

A tutor helped Beverly take the first steps to literacy. The individual attention she received helped her in ways that a traditional classroom setting never could. Now, learning is a central part of her life. "I get too depressed sitting at home doing nothing. When I'm learning and sharing I am happy." When I ask what reading and writing has given her she responds, "I can go places I have never gone before. The feeling is so good it is embarrassing."

I asked her what mattered most to her and she responded with her steady clarity. "For people not to put me down. I am helping myself and others too."

"We learn every day," Beverly adds. She told me about an elderly friend that she would visit and for whom she would read the popular book *The Boxcar Children*. That friend had a heart attack and slipped into a coma. Beverly continued to read to her friend for the next few days until she quietly passed away. A few days later, Beverly received a card in the mail from her friend, thanking her for reading to her. It had been mailed before the heart attack. Beverly took this as a special sign. "I try to help people out as much as I can and don't expect anything in return. I know I get back."

What might she tell a person struggling with illiteracy? "I'd say, there is nothing to be ashamed of. The thing you have to be ashamed of is that you don't do anything about it. You are never too old to learn."

There was a caution that came over me in writing this essay. I couldn't quite put my finger on where the anxiety was coming from. How do you tell Beverly's story? I felt a sense of appropriation. But the answer to my question came from her blue folder. There amongst the pages was an essay Beverly wrote last summer. In ten years she had come from barely being able to read and write to expressing herself with her own words, in her own voice:

My name is Beverly MacKinnon and I would like to tell you about myself. I was born and raised in a small town in Southern Ontario. My parents moved a lot. When I was seven, my sister and I went to live with my grandparents. I did not live with my parents again until I was fifteen. I finished grade ten in an opportunity class. I enjoyed school a lot, but I did not understand why I couldn't read after I finished school. When I was attending classes I knew I had problems with reading so I got a friend to help me. I would understand the work but I could not read the work. I think the reason why I passed was because they wanted me to stay with my peer group. I stayed in school until I finished Grade 10. I found that the only type of jobs I could get was washing dishes or cleaning—mostly physical work. I decided to move to Edmonton in 1980 because wages were a lot better than in Ontario. Also a lot of my friends were moving out west.

The first problem after moving was going down to the Employment Office and telling them why I moved to Edmonton. I told them about my reading disability. The gentleman I was speaking with was very disrespectful and unkind. He told me that I should go back to where I came from. I felt hurt, rejected, stupid and very disappointed.

Later that day, I took a friend with me and he helped me fill out a job application. The same day I had an interview at a private sports club. The interviewer gave me a brochure to read but I could only recognize a few words. I asked for a trial period of two weeks as a housekeeper. He said that I could begin work on the night shift—11 p.m. to 7 a.m. He must have liked my work. After two weeks, I was given a raise.

Over the years, I have had to face many difficulties such as getting around on the bus (not knowing how to read maps) or buying special cards for people I cared about. I also found it fairly difficult when people around me were reading the newspaper and I couldn't. I was relying on people around me instead of dealing with my own problem. I did try to attend night school, but I found it was in a typical school, and I didn't do well learning in a group. I really dislike it when people tell me that I am not able to do things, so I set out to prove them wrong. An example of this is when I was told that I would never get a learner's driving permit. I took night classes with a friend and to most people's astonishment I got my learner's license!

When I was introduced to Project Adult Literacy Society (P.A.L.S.) by my physician, I was so happy that this was a one-on-one program. That was ten years ago. It was very hard for me at first, but the tutors that were helping me were very patient and understanding about my disability. While I was at P.A.L.S., they asked me to participate in a radio interview about the program. I did this with my tutor and enjoyed it, but I was very nervous.

During that time I began another literacy program. The Adult Literacy Centre (Prospects) offered a course on book writing, which I took. After that I wrote several children's stories and some poems. The stories were made into an illustrated book at Prospects. I worked on six or seven different children's books, but I am not published yet. I had a story accepted by the Edmonton Journal, but before the publication date that column was cancelled. I also started a math class. In this class I had the chance to improve my skills and help other students who were having difficulties. When I finished reading my first book by myself, I cried. I really enjoy reading now. I have attended about five different literacy conferences. I went to these conferences to learn new ways to help my daughter and myself.

In 1988 my husband and I found out that we were having a baby. I also was now not able to do physical work because of an accident so I decided to work on my brain.

When my daughter was in grade one, she would tell her teacher not to give her anything to take home to read because her mom couldn't read. This really upset me. I thought that I had to better myself to help my daughter with her schooling. I didn't think I had anything to offer because of my disability, but the more I worked at my classes the more confident I became. I found that I volunteered a lot more and gave myself challenges such as reading my books to the children at my daughter's school.

I found that the more steps I made, the more confidence I had to handle more situations, such as being on the Students for Students Steering Committee at P.A.L.S. I am also on the Board for Student Voices for Students.

I find that my family, friends and teachers compliment me on my improvement time and time again. In November 2004, my tutor and very good friend Dawna-Lynn asked me to read the prayer of St. Francis of Assisi at her wedding. Although honoured, I felt overwhelmed that she asked me. To feel more confident, I took P.A.L.S.' public speaking course. I was nervous in front of 170 people at the wedding, but I was complimented over and over for the great job I had done. To think that ten years ago, I could never have done that!

I feel that my new confidence has made it a lot easier to talk to people, and now I can help the people around me without doubting myself. If I do have a problem, I don't feel bad for asking for help. I feel comfortable with the life that I now have, and am eager to continue learning and improving my skills.

This year I was nominated for the P.A.L.S. Student Achievement Award. This was the first year that P.A.L.S. gave this award. I won! I was so shocked, *proud and excited, but deep down I know I deserved it. All my hard work and all the stepping stones have finally paid off.*

Having gone through my own challenges in life, I know I can support my daughter and help her learn. I find it's good for students to see that adult learners sometimes have the same problems they have. I know that it is never too late to fix a problem, no matter where you are in life. I believe that you should never leave a problem to be solved at a better time; it's not worth it. Jump in and trust that you will be supported and successful!

by
Todd BABIAK

The Director

There is an odd buffer zone between the mini art shows at Capital Ex, Edmonton's giant summer exhibition. People walk through the Art Gallery of Alberta display and look for an exit. But there is no exit, not really.

The temporary walls lead them straight to Felix.

"This way, this way, this way," he says. Felix stands at the entrance of an exhibit sponsored by the Nina Haggerty Centre for the Arts, an Edmonton organization that provides creative outlets for people with developmental disabilities. Felix is affiliated with the Nina Haggerty Centre as an artist and as a volunteer—a public relations juggernaut.

There are two directions once people meet Felix. He ushers them with gestures reminiscent of the splashing of water. Splash water left, splash water right. "You want out? This is the Nina Haggerty Centre. You want some information? There's a craft table."

Felix DuBourdieu-Greig is 22-years old. Even though he rode his bike across the city, from Westmount to Northlands, his sandy hair is fashionably messed. He wears denim shorts and a T-shirt. He has a vital, authoritative manner about him, and his eyes smile constantly. Felix is the sort of person you want to impress.

The clients of Capital Ex are weary. It is a sweltering thirty-four degrees on the grounds, a collection of carnival rides and deep fried food. Here inside the SportEx, the lights are strategically low. People wander toward Felix and he answers their questions before they ask. They can go right or go left. There is a bunch of art up on the wall, if they care to look at it. Do they want to know anything about the artists?

Even though the footprints on the concrete floor of the SportEx show the way out of the Art Gallery of Alberta and the Nina Haggerty Centre, many people remain bewildered. Felix patiently directs them on their way.

"No," he says, "it's confusing, and dark. Take your time!"

Felix came to Canada with his mother from Glasgow, Scotland, when he was six-years-old. When he entered the school system, in Edmonton, he was diagnosed with pervasive developmental delay and mild autism. His experiences in elementary school both scarred Felix and inspired him.

"People laughed at me and made fun of me a lot," he says. "And when I see someone being laughed at now, like someone in a wheelchair with no arms, and I say why are you laughing? How would you feel if that was you?

"When I was younger I used to have lots and lots of anger problems. But I know about it now, and understand it."

Felix, like many 22-year-olds, has a busy and adventurous life. He rides his bicycle all over the city. He plays basketball whenever possible. He volunteers for the Nina Haggerty Centre, and he is a practicing artist. During the school year, he harnesses the power of his past experiences—the positives and the negatives—and applies his enthusiasm at Edmonton's Grosvenor School.

"I volunteer there by helping the janitor out and stuff. But mostly I help teachers in the classrooms, with Spanish and stuff. And during recess. There was this kid, maybe grade five or grade six, and he had anger problems. Like me. So I knew how to help him."

Felix interrupts his story to fiddle with the DVD player on a table just inside the exhibit space. He hands out two pamphlets on the Centre, and directs a family toward the exit. The Nina Haggerty Centre, he tells people, is a place where everyone is welcome to make sculptures, canvasses, pottery. When the traffic stops, he continues.

"I walked the kid up and down the hall until he calmed down. You know, you always calm down, no matter how bad it is. And whenever there's a fight in the school I walk in there and break it up. I say, okay, let's figure this out: how did this fight start? I don't have a middle name so I make safety my middle name. I go around the schoolyard and look for broken glass, loose boards, any nails sticking out."

Like most people, Felix would like to make a living doing what he loves. "I want to work with kids somehow. I don't care how."

There is a break in crowd flow, so Felix sits down with a couple of young girls. There is a craft table set up, as part of the exhibition. The girls are timid, so Felix helps them get started on popsicle stick architecture. His fellow volunteer, Victoria Anger, watches Felix with a smile. Victoria has known Felix for years, at the Centre and at camps for the developmentally disabled.

"He's just an awesome guy, so bright and so social. He's very aware of his feelings, which is rare in anybody, and he's sensitive to people. No matter what, he adapts to the situation. He's very intuitive. At camp, if ever there was someone who needed help, who needed a buddy, Felix was always chosen to be the buddy."

Victoria nods and watches him interact with the girls for a while. Felix knows we're talking about him and looks up, and back down at the popsicle sticks.

"Felix doesn't stay inside himself," Victoria says. "He's very creative in how he thinks, how he talks, how he does art. There's not a mean bone in his body. He's got a great relationship with his family, a very equal relationship with his family. You know what I mean?"

Felix's mother, Yvonne DuBourdieu, is a filmmaker and founder of Edmonton's Arthouse Productions. He is a burgeoning director himself, a member of a cooperative of filmmakers who have developmental disabilities. His cooperative is currently making a film about a community garden in downtown Edmonton. Felix shares directing duties with his colleagues.

As an artist at the Nina Haggerty Centre, Felix was also featured in his mother's film *Through the Eyes of Artists*, and travelled to Ottawa for a meeting with author John Raulston Saul. He has also travelled to the capitals of Europe, to Disneyland, and across Canada.

"It's hard, to find time for everything I like to do," he says during another slowdown in pedestrian traffic through the exhibit. "In my spare time I like to draw weird cartoons. I'm really getting into that. It's hard to explain. But after Capital Ex, what I really have to do is get a job and find a new apartment."

Felix has lived on his own for two years. For a while he lived in a group home, with 24-hour staff, but soon realized he would prefer to be alone. So far, he loves it.

Ideally, he would like to secure a career with children, a little janitorial work, with enough time left over for his art, for bike riding, for watching movies, for basketball. He also loves hanging out with his younger brother and sister.

His overall plan is gloriously simple, and attractive. "After I get a job for a while, I guess I'll retire," he says. "And then, I want to travel."

Felix had a girlfriend for a while but it didn't work out, which he says is for the best. He's not discouraged, though. "I'd like to find someone nice, friendly, beautiful. Someone that likes to laugh, goof around, likes my jokes, my artwork. In the future, we'll get married and have kids."

The summer, Felix's favourite time of year, isn't long enough for everything he wants to do. He loves the Edmonton Folk Music Festival, and the Fringe Theatre Festival. But things are so hectic; he's been so busy volunteering at the Capital Ex, for example, that he hasn't had time to get on the rides. His favourite is the Gravitron, a UFO that glues its riders to the back as it spins ridiculously fast. Why does he like the Gravitron so much? The answer seems obvious: everyone knows the Gravitron is awesome.

The galleries go completely quiet. For the time being, there are no Capital Exers. Felix sits back down with the little girls, whose popsicle stick houses have progressed nicely. He offers tips and starts his own creation. I tell him that I was always a poor artist, as I was so afraid to make mistakes I couldn't get started.

"That's not right," he says. "Nobody's bad. Everybody's good, right? Come on, sit down, give it a try."

by
Caterina EDWARDS

Dancing Apart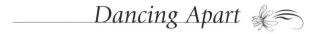

Lindsay Biehn dances apart, separated by a stretch of ice from the rest of her group. The other female participants and volunteers in the Special Olympics skating program, including her mother and younger sister, are clustered in two ragged lines down the centre of the rink. They all face forward, even the triangle of girls in front who lead the others through a dance-skate version of the Macarena. Lindsay is turned away, at a 90° angle, but she moves without hesitation and in time to the music: one hand then the other, on head, shoulders, bottom, a full-body shimmy then a one-quarter-turn jump.

The Macarena is a carefree interlude in the last skating practice of the winter season. The head coach is away, and the year-end show took place a week ago. Earlier in the evening, the thirteen Olympians, male and female, skated under extended arms, stopped suddenly, froze in dramatic positions, then swooped past and around each other, all to the bouncing strains of *Living La Vida Loca*. Earlier too, Lindsay performed both her solo and her pairs skate for me. She handled the elements easily, the circles and the spirals, her strides smooth and strong. The coach choreographed the moves, but Lindsay's shoulder rolls and hand gestures, her interpretations of the music were all hers. And in the pairs, which she skated with a helmeted young man to the music from *Love Story*, she was obviously the one leading.

"Lindsay always knows her steps," comments the mother of one of the other young women with Down syndrome. "Unlike some of the others, she never forgets."

"I'm impressed," I tell Cathy Biehn, Lindsay's mother, during the break. I don't add that despite numerous tries, I never learned to skate. Or that though both of my daughters took lessons, one can skate forward, back, and stop, while the other says she can do forward and "sort of" back.

"Lindsay loves to perform," says Cathy, who is an avid skater herself. "But she wouldn't be able to skate if I hadn't persisted. We started her when she was three. And it was painful at first. I had to hold her up for the longest time."

The skating has long been a Biehn family project. Lindsay's father, Bruce, has faithfully attended the years of practice, cheering her on from the stands. Cathy has volunteered for all of the eleven years that Lindsay has participated in Special Olympics skating, and Lindsay's sister Shawna has coached the group for six of them, beginning when she was only eight years old. Shawna intends to continue working although Lindsay has announced that this is her last year with Special Olympics.

Lindsay is a pretty young woman with a shy and serious manner. She has small, even features, set off by an up-to-date, layered haircut and unobtrusive eyeglasses. Down syndrome is visible only in the fold of her eyelids and her short, stocky stature.

From the beginning, Lindsay's parents felt she should be treated like any other child and be allowed to try everything she wanted to try. She went to an early intervention pre-school with her older sister Angela and some of the neighborhood children. When she started grade school, she attended regular classes, accompanied by a teacher's aide. "Down's kids like to imitate," Cathy says. "It's good for them to be with normal kids, who can act as role models."

During Lindsay's childhood, the Biehns lived in Saskatoon. When she was eleven, they moved to Sherwood Park, which turned out to be a lucky choice. The town has excellent programs for students with disabilities and a support agency, the Robin Hood Association. From junior high on, Lindsay attended a partially integrated program that mixed academic and special life skills classes. In high school, she worked at Cinema City and at a Wendy's fast food restaurant. She also volunteered at a daycare. At present, she has a job one morning a week at a bowling alley in Sherwood Park. She has a written list of tasks, like cleaning tables and filling ketchup bottles, that she's expected to complete. "I like my job," she says.

"She gets over minimum wage, but she doesn't really care how much money she makes," her mother says. "She rarely spends it. She leaves it in the bank." Lindsay also works at a sheltered workshop; currently they are assembling cutlery into packages for airlines. The pay there is more of a token. "Lindsay views it as a social activity," Cathy adds. "Something she does with her friends."

The most difficult time for Lindsay and her family was when she was eight years old and diagnosed with diabetes. She could not understand what it meant: why she could not eat what she wanted, and why she had to have so many needles. Cathy and Bruce had to hold her down in order to administer the insulin. Now, Cathy still measures out the medication and monitors her daughter for symptoms of low blood sugar, noting when she is unresponsive. But Lindsay tests her own blood and self-injects five times a day, having learned how at diabetes camp. Without prompting, she watches her diet. During the break at skating practice, I notice that she takes one sip of the juice she's been given. She puts it down. "I shouldn't drink this," she says. She also exercises daily. Besides skating, she walks an exercise track and bowls in another Special Olympics program. She also performs with Black Light Theatre and, best of all, takes a dance class at the Sherwood Park Robin Hood Centre.

Lindsay loves to dance to pop music. For years, she danced alone in her room, moving and shaking to the cheerful rhythms of Shania Twain or the more driving beats of In Sync and Back Street Boys. "The dancing comes from her heart," Cathy says, comparing it to Lindsay's skating. "She had a couple of years of ballet when she was five and six, but that's all." If anyone walks into her room while she is dancing, Lindsay stops. She doesn't want to be watched. Yet, at the hip hop dance class, she shows no sign of shyness, not even when a TV reporter and a cameraman from a local station arrive to film the session for a news program.

The hip hop class, now in its fourth year, drew media interest when the group appeared in the show *Hip Hop for Hope*, a fundraiser for the Stollery Children's Hospital. "The audience went crazy over them," Vicki, the teacher, tells me. The reaction is also strong every year at the dance competition where they perform (and are awarded a gold medal) without actually competing, and at the annual show in Tofield that Vicki organizes for all of her students.

Watching the four men and four women slamdance to Justin Timberlake's *Good Foot* is a delight. I laugh out loud—with pleasure and, yes, surprise. "We can do it," the lyrics repeat endlessly over a pile-driving beat. "Ain't nothing to it." The hip hop moves suit them: the posing, the strutting, the oversized gestures, and splayed finger signs, the atmosphere of almost-out-of-control energy. The routine does not project the usual hip hop emotions of anger, aggressiveness, or sexuality; instead the dancers radiate confidence and fun.

Before the third run-through, Vicki hands out bright yellow, long-sleeved T- shirts, uniforms for the upcoming performances. This time, instead of modeling the moves for the group, she stands back and watches the routine. 'Oh my goodness," Vicki says at the end, "all the girls need sports bras, firm sports bras."

Lindsay excels in each of the run-throughs. Her steps are cleaner, sharper, more precise than those of the others. When she is not performing, she tends to be quiet and unobtrusive. Before the class, several of the other dancers had come up and introduced themselves. They asked me why I was there. In contrast, during my visits with Lindsay, she answers my questions but doesn't initiate conversation. Even at home, she likes spending time alone, enjoys having the house to herself. But when it comes to performing, Lindsay is a leader. After the hip hop rehearsal, she, her dance partner Tony and another couple, practice a cheerful and bouncy swing dance routine. Again, she is the most aware and accomplished dancer on the floor. She directs Tony with little head and hand signals, reminding him where he should be or which step comes next.

Performing is a way for Lindsay to legitimately claim attention and make her presence felt. It gives her permission to show her true self. As Cathy says about the dancing, "That's Lindsay. That comes from her." And, of course, an appreciative response from an audience encourages her. It helps her to feel accepted.

At the end of the class, Lindsay stands with several of the dancers, "hanging out." One of the young men, Jeff, has an arm around her. She looks relaxed, pleased, although the others are teasing her. She is still flushed from dancing, and someone suggests she is blushing because of male attention.

"I am not," she says. They act like any other group of boys and girls; the only difference is that they behave and speak as if they were in their early teens, rather than their actual age, which is a decade older.

In April, Lindsay will move out of the family home. Although she generally does not like change, she is eager to move into the assisted living co-op apartment that she will share with two other young women, plus staff to guide them and to monitor her diabetes. Several of her friends from Robin Hood left their family homes for such a co-op a year or two ago. And her older sister moved out at Lindsay's current age, twenty-three, so her mother suggests, "She thinks it is the right time for her too."

She will take her bedroom furniture, TV, and the DVD player that she bought with money she earned. She'll also take her multitude of CDs and DVDs. When she likes a film or TV program, she will watch it over and over until she has memorized all the lines. In the last few months, the complete set of *Friends* episodes has been her favored viewing. I wonder if the program about the six unmarried pals provides some sort of model for Lindsay, a fantasy of how things should be.

Lindsay is ready to go off in her own direction. "I'm going to miss her," Bruce says. "She'll be close to us and we'll see her a lot, but I'll still miss her. She seems to be the happiest to see me when I get home."

"I was twenty-five when she was born," Cathy tells me. "Bruce and I thought our lives were over." They discovered that this was not so. They have a life. And with a little help, so does Lindsay.

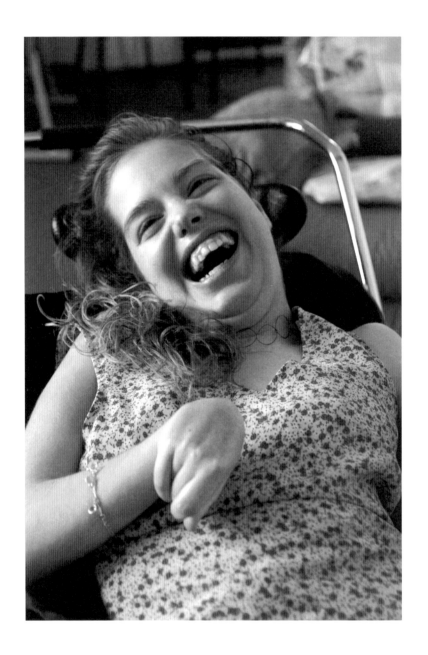

by
Gary HOLDGRAFER

An Expressive Life

Michelle Becker was not expected to live beyond infancy.

"You might find her gone in her crib," the doctor said to Beverly Duff-Simmons, her mother.

Chelle (as she is known to everyone) was born with cerebral palsy. She had a stroke at age four and has had ongoing, sometimes life-threatening battles with pneumonia. She cannot talk or walk. Her hands are so severely contracted that she cannot use them. Chelle is fully dependent upon her caregivers and spends most of her time in her wheel chair. She is now twenty-six years old, having survived overwhelming obstacles.

Twenty years ago, Chelle's parents made the difficult decision to place her in a group home because of the extent of her personal care needs. Chelle now shares her home with three others who also have severe developmental disabilities. A team of caregivers attends to their daily needs and provides a daily schedule of activities for them.

Chelle's family has maintained a close relationship with her. She is the oldest of three daughters born to Beverly and her first husband, Gordon. Although they parted years ago, they are friendly and stand together in making decisions about their daughter's needs. They each visit Chelle on a regular basis. Her dad lives near her in Edmonton while her mother travels from the nearby community of Fort Saskatchewan.

Both parents have re-married and Chelle now has a half-sister, two stepbrothers, and a stepsister, in addition to her two sisters. All are included in her life in some way, along with grandparents and aunts. Her two sisters are frequent visitors, taking Chelle for walks or shopping, decorating her room, or singing to her. Other family members regularly celebrate holidays and birthdays with Chelle.

I first meet Chelle on a mild winter afternoon. Her home is located in a residential neighborhood on the south side of Edmonton. I walk up the long wheelchair ramp to the front door. Mina, one of Chelle's longtime caregivers, invites me into a large and tidy living room.

Chelle lies in the center of the room in her wheelchair, hands tucked in a fixed position on her chest. She has light, sandy brown hair, tied in a ponytail and deep blue eyes framed by long, thick eyelashes. Her complexion is clear and smooth and she is neatly dressed in comfortable, loose-fitting clothes.

Reclining is the most physically comfortable position for Chelle, explains Mina. Chelle turns her face towards me, smiles and makes sounds with her voice. She does not focus on me directly, and I learn later that Chelle is legally blind.

Mina bends over and gently explains to Chelle that I am there to visit her. It is a strange visit, however. Since Chelle cannot talk, I have to ask Mina my questions. All the while, Chelle lies quietly nearby, listening to our conversation, smiling and making sounds whenever Mina speaks to her. It is clear that Chelle enjoys being around Mina.

Mina describes Chelle as "her princess," a happy person. This is a comment that will be repeated by her mother Beverly and by Keri (the team leader at the residence) during my next visit. That takes place a few weeks later. This time, it is early evening. All the residents of the house are present, as well as Eva, another caregiver.

We sit at the dining room table, next to the kitchen, chatting while Chelle lies in her wheelchair next to her mother. Other residents sit at the table with us. Eva attends to them while occasionally adding her own observations to the conversation. Another resident with whom Chelle has a close friendship stands, protectively holding her hand.

We talk for hours. Chelle quietly listens without interrupting, but quickly lights up with a big smile or laughs in response to any teasing or affectionate comments made by her mother. Keri comments that Chelle is sensitive to others and will adjust her mood to match the seriousness or playfulness of a situation. Beverly is quick to add, with a smile, that while that might be true here, Chelle expects to be the center of attention when she comes to her house for a visit. She describes Chelle as always happy at home, often laughing or making sounds to get her mother's attention, even when she is busy.

According to Keri, Chelle brings joy to the group home atmosphere as well as a sense of humour. She is a "prankster" who will kick water on a caregiver during bath time, make a mess that creates extra work, and then laugh. She gets especially tickled when others get into trouble. Keri believes that this is motivated by Chelle's sense of playfulness. She describes her as a "pure soul" who never intends any meanness towards others.

I think back to my first meeting with Chelle and how she smiled so broadly at me when I spoke to her. I remember feeling pleased at how quickly and easily we seemed to bond. Now I wonder if she is really just laughing at me, thinking of a prank she might play. Suddenly, I have an understanding of what others appreciate so much about her. She does not let people take themselves too seriously or too negatively— including herself.

Chelle's happiness appears to be the long-term, enduring kind. It differs from the episodes of momentary happiness that we all experience and which serve to distract us temporarily from the on-going worries and anxieties of daily living. As I get to know her, it is ironic to me that she— and others like her—are often compared to a "norm" or standard in order to determine the extent of their developmental disabilities, when she herself has clearly set the bar for happiness.

Of course, Chelle experiences emotional highs and lows. Keri explains that her sadness and tears communicate physical discomfort, a need for social contact and attention, as well as her longing for absent friends and family members. She will often shriek in delight upon their return. Chelle also lets people know when she is unhappy with them. If her mother is late for a visit, she expresses her anger by being unfriendly.

Chelle experiences occasional depression, usually in the springtime. The reason for this is unclear. She may suffer from seasonal allergies at that time of year. The return of good weather may also make her feel her limitations more keenly. Whatever the reason, given the challenges she faces, it is not surprising that she might feel discouraged now and then.

Fortunately, Chelle's periods of depression are short-lived. She craves excitement and "likes being in the middle of things, in busy environments, and high energy places," says Keri. On those occasions when Chelle's health allows her to go out into the community on day trips, she is unhappy when she has to return to the group home. She cries in disappointment, in Keri's words, with "big tears and a big lip."

Chelle's health has steadily improved since she had a feeding tube inserted into her upper abdomen two years ago. In the years before, she often choked when trying to eat or drink, making it difficult for her to consume sufficient food. Now Chelle receives all of her nutrition through the tube. While she misses eating a range of favourite foods, including sour cream, catsup, chocolate, and last, but not least, brussel sprouts, she has accepted the change without apparent complaint. "She understands that she no longer has to struggle to eat," Keri explains.

Beverly believes that since Chelle's health has improved, her personality has blossomed. She has shifted from being quiet and withdrawn to outgoing. "I thought Chelle would have been my bookworm if she was normal, and now I wonder if she would be part of the bar scene, dancing the night away," she jokes. "Her spirit has definitely come alive."

Chelle is, however, seen as a very responsible resident in her home. She will let staff know when the stove timer has gone off and participates in daily chores such as holding folded towels during laundry time. Keri says that Chelle likes taking part in those activities.

She is also like other young women her age. "She likes girlie things, makeup, jewelry and new clothes," Eva says, "and boys." Chelle decides each morning what she will wear for the day, turning her head away from what is offered to her, until just the right outfit appears in the hands of a caregiver.

One of Chelle's favourite activities is shopping. This often includes a trip down the perfume aisle. She also makes regular stops at the pet store because of her love of animals, including snakes. She loves listening to music and hears very well, based on her response to different kinds of music. Beverly says that she listens quietly to classical music, often played to prepare her for bedtime. She smiles at the sound of Rod Stewart's gravelly voice, and is full of giggles anytime she hears country or easy rock music, especially if others begin to sing along. She once met Raffi, who sang to her. Beverly says Chelle was wide-eyed with a huge smile.

It is clear that caregivers and members of Chelle's family are deeply attached to her, and she to them. Chelle's happy nature has a very positive impact on others. It is her currency for social transactions and she continues to invest it in her relationships. "She is not a chore to care for," Kerri noted. "She gives me more that I give her."

When I first met Chelle and realized the extent of her disabilities, I worried about what I would be able to write about her. What would I say about someone who was unable to talk and tell me about herself? How would I give voice to a story she could not tell? I need not have worried.

"She makes it really easy to see the person, rather than the disability," Keri says.

She is right. All it takes for me to see and learn about Chelle is a curiosity and a desire to make sense of her life. After visiting her, and talking with caregivers and her mother, I am struck by how much there is to say. Chelle has made herself matter to others through the nature of her personality and in the various ways that she has contributed to the tight-knit community in which she lives.

I will continue to reflect on my experience of meeting Chelle, and those who care so deeply for her. If I never see her again, I know that she will revisit me in my memory. There will be none of the "out of sight, out of mind" that has been an unfortunate part of the history for persons with developmental disabilities. She has definitely given me more than I have given her.

Near the end of my second visit to Chelle's home, I hear optimism about Chelle, expressed most clearly in a single word. That word is "future." Keri talks about a future plan for her. Beverly expresses faith in Chelle's health and longevity, after years of saying the same prayer in many times of crisis, "take her now or stop this."

Chelle wasn't taken. Instead, she survives and in her own way, flourishes. My wish is that those who read about Chelle will recognize just how great an achievement that was. Perhaps the next time they see someone with a severe disability, they will pause to wonder about the meaningful personal story that could be told about that person. They may even attempt to reach out and get to know him or her. In doing so, they will learn that each person really matters. Just like Chelle.

by
Allison KYDD

Sidelining

Leslie Murrell has been looking out for himself for as long as he can remember. Now twenty-seven, he says: "I've dealt with ADHD [Attention Deficit Hyperactivity Disorder] since I was five years old. I was the one who noticed that I had a problem, before my parents did. That's kind of how smart I was at the time. From day one I protected myself—mentally, physically, whichever way I had to. I knew from the age of five that I had to."

Not that he didn't have his supporters. "There were a couple of teachers that reached out, that I grabbed onto, that helped me out over the years," he says. There was also a school police officer who saw behind the hardcore façade. "She realized what kind of person I was…actually noticed what I was about," says Murrell.

For the most part, however, most adults didn't know how to help Leslie deal with his problems. "They try and shelter you…like you can't handle [anything]," says Murrell. "They don't really allow you to do anything. Like if you burn yourself, then it's 'Oh, my God, my God.' They try and bandage you up before you even have a cut in your hand."

He continues: "If they [thought] you couldn't learn," he says, "they wouldn't spend time with you. If they thought you *could* learn, they'd spend lots of time with you. It [also] depended on whether the teacher liked you or not." No matter how old he was, Murrell would usually be placed in a grade four classroom. "Even in the high school it was grade four," he says.

Murrell remembers coming to school drunk, finishing his assignments and being told "do whatever you want to do." He put his feet up on the desk, his head back against the wall, and went to sleep. Murrell is scornful of teachers who allowed him to act this way while still placing a token "satisfactory" on his report card.

Having so little expected of him led to what Leslie Murrell calls "mental sidelining, off-track-ness, keeping yourself away from what you should be doing, the goals you should be working on." It also led to feeling he really "wasn't as smart as anybody else," a feeling that's been hard for him to let go of, although he believes he knows better now.

"People with ADHD—they're actually smarter than most people," he says, with more than a trace of bravado. "[They're] not your regular people. Though they're very smart, they play dumb, kind of to test people."

It's difficult to diagnose ADHD and there is no quick cure for the condition. "You have to work with it naturally," says Murrell. "Pills and medication do not work."

He's made a point of learning about his condition and describes it in everyday terms. "'Deficit' is disengaged thoughts," he says. "[An idea] catches and goes the wrong way, or stops in its track and doesn't go anywhere, like a tuning inside your head that one minute grabs and the next minute there's nothing there…You could be in a seminar and only catch about half of what's going on."

Besides the teachers who reached out to him, Murrell says lots of kids in high school "looked up" to him. He had a reputation for being tough and "pretty much ran the school." That didn't last long. First he was expelled for fighting, then for having "some sort of firearm." He changed schools every six months or so while teachers and principals tried to figure out where he belonged. Murrell often made the decision for them, leaving schools whenever he decided "I don't have to be here." Eventually there was nowhere left to go.

"I'm one of your bad apples," admits Murrell. He's been into drugs, lived on the street, worked for an escort service. "I've seen some things nobody should have to see," he says.

Leslie Murrell's parents live in Edmonton, and he has a brother and a sister, although he's not close to them. In fact, he's critical of his parents, whom he feels weren't there for him when he wanted to talk about his future. "I needed more of 'what's going to happen when I get to move out of house and home?'" he says. "[But] it was never really brought up." When he decided to leave and they said, "No, don't move, don't move, stay here," it was too late.

With the help of SKILLS—an organization that supports and advocates for people with developmental disabilities—Murrell now has a regular job "filling boxes with supplies and shipping them off." He finds the work boring and repetitive. More important is his desire to become an actor and a comedian. "I know I've got what it takes," he says. And these aren't just dreams. In the last two years he's had some practical theatrical training and experience.

That training was provided by director, writer, drama coach and teacher Gerry Potter, founder of Workshop West Playwrights' Theatre. In Murrell's words, "Gerry's been a God-send. He brought the acting out of me…He treats me as an individual, not someone who's got a disability. He treats everybody else with respect, but with me…it's more of an actor-to-producer relationship."

Murrell describes how the opportunity came about. "There were a few of us—SKILLS was looking for a way to get us out of the house," he says. After consulting with parents, staff, people who work in theatre and self-advocates, the society came up with the idea of a theatre company. In the fall of 2004, Rising Sun Theatre was formed specifically to accommodate people with disabilities, and Potter was hired to do a weekly workshop. He took participants on field trips, taught them theatre skills, games and exercises.

Potter had to be especially creative because of the wide range of abilities in the group. "Some came and went," he says, "but most stayed." They were interested in doing a play, but there were no suitable scripts available, so he wrote one to fit the group. For Leslie Murrell he created the character of Anansi, a trickster spider-man. The play, *The Giraffe Who Thought He Could Fly*, became a half-hour production. In June 2005, it was presented at Edmonton's Arts Barns and later, at the Saskatoon Fringe Theatre Adventures. Though the production featured actors with disabilities, Potter was no babysitter. He expected his actors to turn up and be prepared to work.

This year Potter continues to work with the group, although it's essentially a volunteer position. There is no funding, but SKILLS provides rehearsal space and any additional support it can. "Hopefully, some grant money will come through," says Potter. "Right now, we're going along on good will." He believes in the project. "The people in the group gain a lot from it," he says. "They're growing in a lot of ways, and so am I. When you focus on what people can do rather than what they can't do, there are surprises."

This year, the group is creating a show based on personal experiences. "It's a tough thing, the discipline of putting a show on," says Potter. "It's all about teamwork," and participants "try to honour each other." This echoes what Murrell has said about being treated with respect. Murrell is part of the group, but Potter works with him individually as well. "He's quite capable of a lot of things," says Potter, "and wants to create his own show. We're testing that possibility."

In spite of his enthusiasm, Murrell admits he's not ready to make a living through acting, "not yet." "There's lots of theatre in Edmonton, but no money in it," he says. At the same time, he describes himself as "one of Rising Sun Theatre's actors who has turned himself around."

"I mostly have to work with Gerry on his own…was thinking of taking classes, but don't have grade ten," he says. Not having finished school gets in the way a little, but he thinks a combination of natural abilities and a lot of fight will make up for it. "Maybe a little farther along the line I might go back to school."

Another way that Murrell may be able to exploit his acting talents is in comedy. He's been told he's a natural comedian with good timing. He also watches comedy astutely, noting what makes audiences laugh. "If it makes them laugh, sell it; if it doesn't make them laugh…you're doing something wrong…If you want to be a comedian, do something different." Again, he's sure he can do it. "I can make you die laughing; I can make it hurt," he says. "I don't hold back."

Since Edmonton has several comedy clubs, he hopes to hone his skills right here and has his strategy worked out. "In some clubs you have to be careful how you say your swears," he says. "Some clubs, give it all you've got—Yuk-Yuks, they don't care. Comedy Factory, you have to be careful…"

Though he's outspoken in many ways—not to mention bubbling over with braggadocio—Leslie Murrell isn't an easy man to get to know. He doesn't apologize for it. "Geminis talk in riddles," he says. "When you think about Gemini, think of Yin and Yang. This is how my brain works.

There's always two. It's like having an angel on one shoulder and a grim reaper on the other; it's like a battle every day…"

"I don't like to talk very much," he adds unexpectedly. "I've noticed that I'm a very quiet person—sociable, but within a crowd…Basically, I'm a very mellow person," he adds. "I'm one of those guys that will actually sit in a room with a bunch of people and let them all talk first before I even I jump into it. Sometimes I won't even jump in…That's another thing with ADHD actually. We all sit and listen. We don't say [anything] until we get our cue."

He continues: "If people get to know me, they'll know who I am." He admits that he's suspicious of what he calls "emotional crap" and that his reticence has affected his relationships. "A lot of my ex's have tried to get to know me," he says. "I'm not pushy. I don't like clingy people. I don't like people telling me what to do—bossy people. I can't stand them. They drive me nuts—that's called narrow-minded, right?"

Not only does he know what he doesn't like, but he's pretty clear about the kind of relationships he wants. "Everything's got to be equal," he says. "If it's not—I won't do it. I'll actually say that."

Though he can be reserved, Murrell has a wide range of interests. He says he's made a "study" of religion. "I've ripped the Bible apart," he says. "It's all stories. Life is too short to stick to just one thing. My religion is gypsy. My mother was born with the actual gypsy blood in her." His family tree also connects him to Celtic, German and French mysticism, and Rastafarianism.

Interested in movies, Murrell thinks British films are better because they "show everything." He waited a long time to borrow a new release called *Cruel Intentions*. "If you get a chance, watch it," he says, then hesitates, "It's kind of graphic—Playboy graphic." A moment later, he explains his hesitation, "I'm polite that way. I don't want to totally offend [you]," he says. Though some part of him may aim to shock, there's also a side that wishes to please.

Leslie Murrell is also image conscious. He'll happily show you his gold tooth, and he admires dreadlocks. "It's not symbolic, he says. "It's more style than anything. It's more self-preservation style. I'm big time on style—some like short hair; some like long—mine's having dreadlocks."

Perhaps his most significant interest is music. If he wears a Dead Jesus sweatshirt, he's not making a religious or philosophical statement.

"It's a band," he explains. He describes music as "therapy, essential therapy," lists the genres he listens to and describes the differences between them: gothic grundge, heavy metal, gothic rap, alternative/edge. "Gothic, it's more...the way the sounds are—it's kind of mind altering—in the background. They've got stuff that your mind picks up, takes you to another dimension."

Murrell also likes B-tribe ("Celtic/alternative—a lot like Sarah McLaughlin"), rhythm and blues, M&M, Great Malenko, *I Robot* (Bad Boys), ICP (Insane Clown Posse), Twisted Freak Show. His taste is eclectic, but if he catches you playing country, he's liable to say, "Play something that's got some life in it."

Someone this savvy about popular culture is bound to have heroes, and Murrell's are an eclectic group of actors, musicians and stand-ups: Samuel Jackson, Vin Diesel, Triple X, Wesley Snipes, Ad Chandler, Robin Williams (when he's not "cheesy"), Eddy Griffin, Will Smith...

There's little doubt that Leslie Murrell pushes the bounds of what society expects from a person who is intellectually challenged. He won't give up and withdraw from society simply because he has a disability. "God hates a man to be a coward...don't sit back and do absolutely nothing." says Murrell. He'd much rather "come out swinging."

by
Gloria SAWAI

Plus More

I met Imebet Ross for the first time on a windy afternoon in March, at Charles William's Hair Plus More, a salon on Argyll Road, where she works. I had called the salon's owner, Joan Noddings, to set up a hair appointment so I could talk to her about Imebet and also about herself — why she has taken on the challenge of hiring adults with developmental disabilities and what that process has been like.

I was sitting at Joan's station in a small room separate from the main area of the salon, getting a shampoo and set and asking questions about Imebet—what her job entailed, how she got on with clients and other stylists. I had not yet met Imebet herself.

"The clients like her very much," Joan said. "She brings a sense of joy to the salon. She's a delight to have, absolutely wonderful. And she has thrived in this environment, has become more self assured."

"What would you do if a client didn't like her, if they expressed dissatisfaction in some way?" I asked.

"Well, they would no longer be welcome in my salon."

I heard a quiet fierceness in her voice, and I realized that Imebet had a real advocate in Joan. She also told me that Imebet was of Jamaican descent, thirty-seven with the mental capacity a young child, the disability likely caused accidentally at birth.

Then Imebet herself entered the room. She was short, neatly dressed in a clean blue shirt and pressed pants, her black hair pulled back in a single braid. Imebet was carrying a cup of coffee in both hands, and she brought it to me. I took the cup and thanked her. She smiled. I saw the delight she took in serving it. Imebet doesn't know many words, but her eyes and smile speak volumes. She paused beside my chair, looked at my sweater, purple with gold flecks, and laughed.

"A pretty sweater!" she exclaimed.

"Thanks," I said. Then, "Your hair looks nice braided like that."

She smiled but didn't reply.

"Who braids it?" I asked.

"My mother."

She lingered in the doorway, watching—curious, attentive, making no move to leave.

Finally Joan said "Have you folded the towels yet, Imebet?" And she turned, left the room, and went back to work.

Joan Noddings has been hiring adults with developmental disabilities for 14 years, working with them one at a time. Imebet has been with her for seven years. She works three days a week—Wednesday, Thursday and Friday afternoons from one to four. Joan pays her salary, receiving no financial aid from government or private sources.

Selections, an agency that helps people with disabilites find work, placed Imebet at the Charles William's Salon. Linda Crawshaw, a career development coordinator at Selections, helped Imebet get started. To make her job responsibilities clear, Linda has designed a loose leaf binder that contains several pages with coloured pictures of each duty: wash cups, wash towels, dry towels, fold them and put them in the cupboard, sweep the floor, dust the counters, make coffee…Next to each picture is a box to be checked off when the duty is complete. The pages are covered with plastic sheeting and Imebet uses a felt marker to check off her duties. The checkmarks are erased each Friday, so when she comes back the following week she has clean pages to work with. The book is kept on an accessible shelf and Imebet likes to stand in front of it, pen in hand, keeping track of duties completed. She takes pride in her accomplishments. When a stylist suggested she show me her book, Imebet brought it over to me.

"Well, you work hard," I said, turning the pages.

"Yes."

"You do many different jobs."

"Yes."

If someone asks her to do something not listed in the book, she responds with, "That's not my job."

I asked Joan what skills she needed in order to train Imebet for her job. She said it was important to give Imebet clear, consistent, and simple directions. It was also vital to teach her to stay on task.

"And what happens if she doesn't stay on task?"

"Well, we have to remind her. But not harshly or she might start crying. You use a light touch."

A few weeks later, I saw Imebet again. I arrived at the salon at 12:30, when she was eating her lunch before starting work. We sat together in a small room that held a cupboard with counter top and built-in sink, a microwave oven, a table and two chairs, and, in a recessed area, a washer and dryer. Imebet was sitting at the table, eating a cheese sandwich that she'd placed in the microwave so the cheese had melted between the bread slices. She also had a carton of fruit juice and one of yogurt. I asked if I could have a cup of coffee and she said yes. This time she didn't pour. And she didn't smile. Perhaps she realized I was no client and I could get my own. Or more likely, that this was not on her duty list. I poured my own and sat down with her.

"Who made your sandwich?" I asked.

"I did," she said.

"Do you like cheese sandwiches?"

"I like to put it in the microwave and the cheese melts."

She was serious about the topic, not smiling or laughing, her eyes questioning, cautious. I saw that answering questions one-on-one with a stranger did not bring her the joy she showed when she was serving the clients or mingling with the stylists. She was quiet, reserved. I was curious. I already liked her.

"How do you get to work?" I asked.

"By bus."

"Does someone come with you?"

"No, I come by myself."

"One bus?"

"No, two buses."

"You transfer then."

"Yes."

I knew that she lived with her mother and I thought: Imebet has another advocate looking out for her best interests, nurturing her independence—her mother.

When she'd finished her lunch she wiped off the table, threw the empty cartons in the waste bin, and set to work washing cups. She laid a clean towel on the counter and after she'd washed and rinsed the cups, placed them top down on the towel. When I asked if I could help her she shook her head and kept on working. After that, Imebet removed towels from the dryer and started folding them. She folded them carefully and stacked them on the shelf, the way my mother used to do, with the folded edges facing front. When she was finished, she rejoined the group in the salon, sweeping the floor and offering coffee to clients.

Soon I heard her excited laugh. I joined the group in the salon. A young mother had come in with her new-born baby, two weeks old. The stylists had gathered around the infant, admiring it, smiling and laughing. And Imebet most of all. I witnessed first hand what one of the clients had expressed earlier: "This is a little shop with a big heart."

Later, when a woman arrived to pick up a friend, she carried in with her a newborn lamb —not a usual event in any salon—and Imebet fled the scene, standing against the back wall. When I asked her if she liked the lamb, she shook her head and nodded emphatically, "No!" She also doesn't like dogs or cats.

For the most part, Imebet does, however, like people. Most of the stylists have been with Joan for several years, some since the shop opened nineteen years ago. Everyone seems to work well with Imebet and to enjoy her presence. And Imebet clearly enjoys both clients and stylists. With perhaps one exception.

"Do you like everyone who works here?" I asked her.

"Not Dennis."

"Why not?" I asked.

"He's always bugging me."

"Teasing you?"

"Yes."

"You don't like it."

"I don't like it."

"What do you do?"

"I tell Joan."

"What do you say?"

"Dennis is bugging me again."

"What does Joan say?"

"Dennis, quit bugging Imebet."

"And does he stop?"

"Yes."

"Maybe he does that because he likes you."

No answer.

One of the regular clients at the establishment is Mrs. St. Clair. When I first saw her she was sitting under a dryer. When the drying cycle was finished I sat down beside her and asked what she thought of Imebet.

"She's a darling girl," she said. "A happy sprout."

Joan told me later that some clients bring small gifts to Imebet, candy mostly, which she loves, particularly chocolate. She also enjoys the weekly visit of the Nut Man, Kevin, who sells nuts and candy to the stylists and clients who wish to buy, and always has a piece of candy just for Imebet.

Joan's salon is named after her great grandfather, Charles Williams Noddings, who moved to Canada from England in 1886 and settled near Athabasca.

"He was a special man," Joan told me, "a linguist and philologist who knew several languages. He was an internationalist and a man of great hospitality." She showed me some articles about him tacked to the wall in the waiting area. In one of them Joan was quoted as saying, "It is my wish that we at Charles Williams will continue his tradition, caring for our friends and customers." Witnessing the camaraderie among the stylists and clients and the hospitality shown toward everyone, especially Imebet, I saw that her wish has been fulfilled. In 2004, Joan received the Mayor's Award for employers who support and accommodate persons with disabilities in a paid position. She, with eight other employers, received the award at City Hall.

The last time I saw Imebet was on a sunny afternoon in April. This time she was wearing pressed jeans, a fashionable vest, and orange sandals. Her toenails were painted bright red. She was in a playful mood with one of the clients who was waiting for a haircut. The client covered his face with a newspaper and Imebet enjoyed pushing the paper aside and finding his face.

I had set up my appointment for later in the afternoon, thinking that I would take the same bus that she took to go home. It was not such a good idea. When I joined her outside to walk with her to the bus stop, saying I was going home too, she hurried ahead of me, glanced back at me a couple of times with a look of suspicion, and walked faster. I started to feel like a stalker, but it was too late to turn back. She was careful and confident dealing with the busy traffic on 99th Street and Argyll Road. But she walked swiftly, faster than I could keep up.

When the bus arrived Imebet got on, showed the driver her pass and went to the very rear of the bus. I sat near the door. It was a long ride to the Millwoods Town Centre. The bus was hot and dusty, and crowded in the rush hour. When it finally stopped at the terminal she got up and walked out. I stood by the open door and called to her, "Good-bye, Imebet."

She looked back at me.

"Good-bye," she said and hurried across the road to wait for her next ride.

I watched for awhile as she sat on a bench near her transfer stop, the dry wind gusting around her, the sun warm above. And I thought of words like *courage, honesty, pride, humility*.

I also thought of the place where she worked, the Charles William's Hair Plus More Salon. I thought of the good humour and patience of the staff, the respect they show Imebet, expecting good work from her, not condescending in their treatment of her, but acknowledging her accomplishments. And right then I gained a new understanding of what "Plus More" in the salon's name actually stands for.

by
Mark KOZUB

The Cat's Meow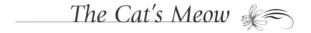

Dan Atkinson looks and acts younger than his years. Although he turns sixty this year, he has the presence of someone vaguely lost in time. His face has few wrinkles and under his moustache of reddish and silver his smile exudes a boyish glow. His clothes add to his youthful appearance. Dan—or "Danny" as his siblings refer to him—wears jeans six inches too long with the bottoms rolled, and from his pant's pocket dangles a keychain with his name on it.

On his sixtieth birthday "Danny" Atkinson will be working, using his wagon to deliver newspapers around his neighbourhood. "Everybody knows me and my wagon." He scratches his head, blinks, and continues. "When I was a kid, everyone else on the block had a little red wagon but poor little old me!" Then he pauses and shrugs his shoulders. "I had everything else, just not a red wagon."

One of the things that Dan had was a disability. He was diagnosed with mental retardation. "My mom and dad didn't even know he had a handicap until he went up to grade four, and then they noticed he was having trouble at school," says his youngest sister Dianne. "He was deprived of oxygen at birth. That sort of thing just doesn't happen anymore."

There were five children in the Atkinson family, Dan the second eldest. Certain memories of his childhood remain utterly clear but sometimes, important details evade him. For example, Dan spent time in

Red Deer's Michener Centre—a training school for "mental defectives"—as a young man. He is not entirely sure when he stayed there, for how long or why. Like his siblings, he suspects his mother and father had their hands full raising a large family and probably didn't know how to care for him.

One thing that Dan definitely remembers is that he wasn't fond of his time at Michener. "It was like a jail," Dan recalls matter-of-factly. "There was a working gang there. You had to be in the working gang. You had no choice. There was a root cellar there where we had to screen potatoes. It's like a wooden square with slots in it and the dirt falls through and the potato stays on top. Thursday nights, we had movie nights where we got to go to the gym and watch movies. Sometimes I couldn't go because they had a star chart on people. If you had three Xs in a row, you couldn't go to movie night."

Although Dan is usually a happy person, painful memories of his youth in the Michener Centre sometimes trouble him. Questions about physical and emotional abuse linger. "I think I went through some of that," Dan admits. "Emotionally especially." Then he smiles. "But the carpentry shop they had there, that was free. You just got to go if you liked it." He grins. "That was something I really liked."

Despite showing some talents as a handyman (perhaps gained from the carpentry shop at the Michener Centre), Dan has troubles with some of the details of day-to-day that many of us take for granted. "Cooking has been a challenge for him. It took him a long time just to operate the stove properly," says Dianne.

"He's not bad on the range," Dan's younger brother Dave, fifty-four, counters. "I think he's quite comfortable with it now."

"Money has always been an issue for him," Dianne adds. "He might be able to count money if he concentrates really hard."

"I think he can count okay," argues Dave. "It just takes him a little longer than the average guy."

"I don't know if he knows how to tell time that well," Dianne continues, "especially not on a clock with hands on it. He always has a digital clock. I know my brothers used to tease him sometimes and ask him what time it was."

While his siblings may argue over the limits of Dan's abilities, they agree that he has come a long way since his days at the Michener Centre. Dan moved into an apartment of his own but still needed a lot of help to manage his life. "Mom basically looked after him," says Dianne. "They'd go to get groceries and she'd pay his bills. There was no such program as Transitions back then. When Mom passed on fifteen years ago, I took over for her and I learned about Transitions and they've been great."

Transitions Rehabilitation Association provides Dan with ongoing supports. His worker Sheylan Thibault spends approximately twenty-five hours each week with Dan. "I mostly teach him healthy eating habits, some personal hygiene, budgeting, banking, and a lot about grocery shopping, that's one of the biggest things. And I'm slowly teaching him to cook," says Thibault. "The work I do with Dan is mostly in his home, plus whatever errands need to be done."

Dan now lives independently in a house that he shares with another man who is disabled. He earns a living from his *Gazette* route, the occasional snow-shoveling job, and income from the Assured Income for the Severely Handicapped (AISH) program. "You couldn't pay me $200 to go back to my old life in the Michener Centre," says Dan. "Now, I can come and go as I please. Doors won't be locked after I leave." His newfound freedom means that he can enjoy a meal or a visit with his family at any time. One topic of conversation that crops up when Dan gets together with his siblings is *Seinfeld*. "We're quite a *Seinfeld* family," says Dianne.

"I love Kramer and George," says Dan. There are other TV shows he loves… "Friends, Home Improvement, Everybody Loves Raymond…" He likes watching movies on TV, too, "like that *Planes, Trains and Automobiles*…except John Candy's dead."

He doesn't watch *Sex in the City*, though, and not because of its racy content. "It's on too late," he says. "I'm up early, at three o'clock in the morning. That was part of the Michener, too. We used to have to be up early, and once you get that biological clock in your head, you can never get it out." He smiles, shakes his head and shrugs his shoulders. "Waking up early. I just got used to it."

On snowy days like the one on which we first met, Dan goes outside with a cup of coffee and a cigarette—the latter being one of his bad habits, he admits—and shovels snow for himself and others. He's proud to mention that he has performed some interesting triage on his damaged snow shovel. "I got one of those back-saver snow shovels, the kind that curves a bit, and the stick got busted in the bend," he explains, "so I took it apart and saved the handle part of it, because that part wasn't busted.

Then I took a hockey stick and cut off the bendy part of it, stuck the handle on there, put a couple of screws in there, and it works like a cat's meow!"

When he's not working, Dan bowls with other Special Olympics athletes or plays on the Special Olympics hockey team. Dan's been with the team for at least five years. "I play defense. I'm pretty average." He explains that he's on the B team, which is better than being on the D team.

"A whole bunch of us get together and play hockey every Tuesday and we get along quite well," explains Chris, one of Dan's teammates. "Dan's a really great guy. I highly respect him for the individual he is. He's a very respectful person. He does a lot of community service. The whole team respects him. He's never missed a hockey practice."

Dan's friend and teammate Dusty, age twenty-four, appreciates Dan's presence too, but for a different reason. "He has a funny laugh," says Dusty, chuckling.

With Dusty and other friends, Dan bowls at the St. Albert Bowling Centre every Saturday. When asked if Dan is a good bowler, Dusty does something with his head. It's between a nod and a shake. "A few strikes," he says.

"I just go there for the fun of it," says Dan. "The first time I went ten pin bowling, the ball almost dragged halfway down the lane! One of my old roommates who was with me, she says, 'Don't SWING the ball, just PUSH it!'"

Through Special Olympics, Dan has made many friends, such as his bowling and hockey buddies "Terry, Phil, Dusty, and Jason... I can't forget about Jason! He keeps givin' me hugs every time he sees me!"

Dan also has a girlfriend, Donna. Their romance blossomed at the Transitions Christmas party in a rather dramatic fashion, the stuff of soap operas or romantic comedies. "She wasn't very happy with the other guy that night," Dan begins. The "other guy" was Donna's previous beau. "She broke up with him that night. Actually, the other guy made her cry. She wasn't very happy with him." Then he smirks. "I just went right in there, hook, line and sinker."

Having a new girlfriend is inspiring Dan to learn more about cooking. He is getting better at making muffins and other baked goods. However, for Valentine's Day, Sheylan prepared the meal for Dan and Donna. "I set the table but she [Sheylan] made the dinner," Dan points out. As it turns out, Dan's tastes in food are not the most romantic. "There's one thing Sheylan won't cook, so she forces me to cook it, eh: liver and onions!" he says, laughing.

When Dan isn't joining his girlfriend on a date, he plays darts at the St. Albert Senior's Centre or simply bikes around the area surrounding his house. He is known by many as a good neighbour. "He's been a great help in the community," says Anita Ferri, whose 21 year-old son lives in a house across the street from Dan. "If we're going on holiday as a family, we'll let Dan know," she says. "When we come back, he'll say, 'I saw such and such car out there for such and such hours.' He's *on* it!"

When Anita sees Dan, she doesn't see his disability. "It doesn't factor at all into our relationship with him," she says. "He comes, he visits, he heads off, he has all those social traits you'd expect in the best kind of neighbour. And I'll tell you: these days, a good neighbour is hard to find."

Dan is creating his own community too: P.I.P. "People In Power," he says loudly. "You know who came up with that? ME!" Currently, there are nine people in the group. It meets once a month. Sometimes, they have guest speakers and go to courses. "We just went to one by the Edmonton Inn on Kingsway Avenue, right across from the Chateau Louis," he broadcasts. Then his voice drops and he pauses to think. "The first day, the Friday, we just got to know everybody. On the Saturday, I didn't go." Then he laughs. "I didn't fully organize the ride for myself."

It is through P.I.P. that Dan is learning how to stand up for himself. "In that first PIP meeting, someone was sitting too close to me. She was bothering me all weekend, touching my leg," he says. "I got up and moved. Instead of being rude, I was quiet about it." Dan is also learning that there are different ways of saying things, of expressing himself without hurting the other person's feelings. "When I was going to the Michener, I couldn't do nothing about my feelings, I just kept it bottled up inside," he says. "I still do that sometimes."

While Dan may often bottle up his emotions, he's hardly quiet about his love of rock music. "*The Bear* is my favourite radio station," he declares. "I tape it with my tape recorder. That's how I picked out most of my CDs, from listening to *The Bear*."

His CD collection is a small but significant shrine to rock legends, some more significant than others. "Trooper! That's one of my favourites!" Dan exclaims. "In the garage, I even have some eight tracks of KISS, including their four solo ones. I'm keeping those. Those will be worth money someday, if you take them into a pawnshop!"

Even though Dan doesn't have an eight track player, the KISS eight tracks will likely remain in his garage. Dan is a packrat. "I've never seen anyone more habitual," says his brother Dave. "His garage is full of old stereos that don't work but he has to hang on to them. It's difficult for him to throw things out."

Dan's pack rat nature extends to his clothes closet. Dianne has to work hard in order to persuade her brother to get rid of old clothes that are too worn or out of fashion. "He has this thing about his clothes," she says. "It can be eighty above outside and he'll wear a T-shirt and a flannel long-sleeve shirt. That's what he wears. It's hard for him to change."

Dan is equally stubborn about giving up smoking. "He doesn't inhale," says Dianne. "He never has. We've been after him to quit, but he's not going to."

Short of paying for cigarettes he doesn't really smoke, Dan is learning to manage his money and be resourceful with what he has. For example, after his nephew across the street was putting hardwood floors into his house, Dan used the spare flooring to craft a cover for the wagon he uses to deliver his papers…and he'll be using that wagon when he's celebrating his sixtieth birthday by working. But Dan doesn't mind. He's proud of his job. And he's proud of his wagon. "It works like the cat's meow," he says.

by
Kalin JENSEN

Two Steps Forward

Michelle Arklie is nineteen years old, running through the streets of Oliver, British Columbia; carrying a flag the same height as she, a wide smile on her face. She is one of six young runners honoured with the task of carrying the flag for a one kilometer leg of the 1990 British Columbia Winter Games. Sixteen years later, her mother Marilyn touches the grainy newspaper photograph commemorating the event. "'Chelle ran a total of one and a half kilometers instead of the one kilometer they told her to run!" she laughs, turning the pages of a dog-eared scrapbook.

Michelle's athleticism is still much in evidence on the day I first meet her. She is sitting on the front stoop of her duplex, a tall, broad-shouldered young woman lounging in the dry heat of an Edmonton summer, her mop of curly orange-red hair shining in the mid-afternoon sun. She can barely suppress her laughter as she watches me hobble towards her on my brand-new in-line skates. I collapse next to her and attempt to free my feet from their bindings. "Do you know how to rollerblade?" I ask. She stands quickly, one hand on the front doorknob. "I can teach you if you want to. I'm really good," she asserts. "No, no, no," I say quickly, "How about after the interview?" Michelle slowly sinks back down onto the step. "Okay, but I'll show you when we're done."

I learn that running and rollerblading aren't Michelle's only hobbies. She is also an avid curler. Her love of the game began when her family lived in British Columbia. Marilyn Arklie—an assistant curling instructor—

enrolled all of her children in junior curling. After the family moved to Edmonton in 1991, Michelle approached David Nedohin, a member of Randy Ferbey's legendary curling team. She asked him to help her lobby for the establishment of a curling team for people with special needs. He told Michelle that he would try his best to get ice time for such a team at the Derrick Club in Edmonton. Eventually ten players were recruited to play, one of whom was Michelle. The group would go on to win a silver medal at the Special Olympics.

Michelle is a passionate advocate for the Special Olympics, often speaking on behalf of the organization on local television programs. Although she has some difficulty in expressing how it felt to win her silver medal, she has no hesitation in asserting that her most memorable moment was meeting curling superstar Randy Ferbey and the other members of his team. When asked what she likes most about the sport, she declares: "I love curling because it's a family heirloom. My family did it and now I'm hooked."

It wasn't always so easy for Michelle to stick with an activity like curling. When she was a child in the 1970s, she had difficulty concentrating on any subject for any length of time. She was diagnosed with Attention Deficit Disorder (ADD). Her mother is uncertain how she would be diagnosed today. Back then, ADD was a blanket diagnosis often given to children who had developmental difficulties of any kind. Looking back, Marilyn Arklie says that she and her husband "knew all along something was different. She wasn't learning as fast as the other kids."

In addition to ADD, Michelle is also epileptic. Her mother says that when she was a baby, Michelle was sometimes unresponsive and had a blank look on her face. At eighteen months old, on the way back from an air show, her head started shaking to one side of her car carrier and her eyes rolled out of focus. Michelle's parents raced her to the hospital, where they were told that the noise from the air show had triggered a grand mal seizure.

From then on, Michelle had to be carefully watched. She had a seizure at least once a month, usually in the form of a petit mal. "I couldn't really leave [Michelle] alone, unless someone else was there to watch her," she explains. "If 'Chelle had more than one seizure, we'd have to pack her into the car and take her to the hospital." In 1991, she was admitted as part of a test program for the drug Frisium. Since using the drug, Michelle has not had a seizure, although there is always a possibility that they might recur.

Despite the challenges, Marilyn and Robert Arklie did everything they could to help Michelle develop as best she could. They enrolled her in speech therapy to help raise her verbal skills to the level of her peers; although Michelle had little difficulty getting her point across in conversation, she consistently left out prepositions and other linking words in sentences. Fortunately, her language difficulties didn't slow her down. She was outgoing and had little trouble socializing with other children her age. Michelle became good friends with a neighbor girl and the two took to playing tricks on their parents. They would eat breakfast at the Arklie's and then go over to the friend's home to eat a secret second breakfast, all before returning to the Arklie's house for lunch.

As the youngest of three children, Michelle was treated like any other member of the family. Her daily chore was to set and clear the table before and after meals. "When Michelle could dress herself, she'd dress herself. When she could feed herself, she'd feed herself." her mother explains. "Whatever we did as a family, we all did together."

When Michelle was ready for public school, she was enrolled in a special education class in which she could learn at her own speed. This changed in high school. There, Michelle was allowed to attend the same courses as people her own age, but was given simpler assignments. For instance, in mathematics, she learned about time, money, and elementary functions while the other students focused on algebra and geometry.

Today Michelle lives in a duplex with two roommates, including her best friend Cathy. She also shares her space with eight rotating support workers from SKILLS, a local organization dedicated to enabling developmentally disabled adults to live independently. The support workers help Michelle with her ironing, grocery shopping, banking and budgeting.

Michelle is supported financially through the Assured Income for the Severely Handicapped (AISH) program and a part-time job at the downtown cafeteria of EPCOR (Edmonton's electrical utility). Two hours each day, she works the lunch shift, refreshing salt and pepper shakers, clearing and washing tables, and checking boardrooms for cleanliness. "I like the people I work with, my boss, and the people who come eat," she explains. She has been employed with the kitchen for the past few years and plans on staying as long as the arthritis in her wrist allows her to do so.

"I am going to move into a condo with Cathy," Michelle says, fiddling with the hem of her shorts. Cathy is about to receive an inheritance from her father and is looking into purchasing a condominium elsewhere in the city. "I need more privacy." A vehicle pulls up to the curb and her two neighbours pile out, walking toward the adjacent duplex unit which is also aided with SKILLS' support.

"Hi, Michelle. Hi, hi, hi, hi!" one of her neighbors calls out.

"Hi," Michelle responds with exasperation in her voice. "Can you give me some time please? I'm doing an interview right now." She turns back to me as her neighbours enter their side of the duplex. "I don't have enough privacy. Me and Cathy are more independent."

Michelle and Cathy have been planning this move for three years. However, there are a few obstacles blocking their path. One of these is Michelle's difficulty understanding the importance of personal health and safety. Charlotte Sabourin, Michelle's primary support worker, explains that Michelle "puts herself at risk and doesn't realize she's doing it. She needs someone around to remind her to focus on activities like cooking. She won't cook meat all the way. She can burn her hand by forgetting the burner is on." Charlotte helps Michelle with activities by clearing the room of distractions and reminding Michelle to pay close attention to the activity at hand.

If Michelle does manage to move into an apartment with Cathy, it will be two steps forward to independence, one step back. The pair will have their own home but will still need support, albeit on a reduced level. Staff will only be present at the home during the day and on-call overnight. Support will then be increased or decreased, depending on the progress of the two women. Despite these caveats, Cathy and Michelle look forward to the day when they will finally gain the limited privacy that they desire.

When Michelle has answered the majority of my questions, I strap my in-line skates back on my feet and ask her if she is still willing to give me that lesson on how not to fall flat on the pavement. She runs inside and brings out her skates, a helmet, and pads for every place on your body that could possibly be injured in a fall. I make a mental note that perhaps I should invest in a few of those pads myself. Soon we are gliding down the street. Michelle skates easily along, an impressive feat given the physical and developmental challenges that she has faced throughout her life. I recall an earlier conversation with her mother, in which I asked her to name the accomplishment of Michelle's that made her most proud as a parent. "[Michelle has done] lots of things that are impressive," said Marilyn Arklie. "Just being able to go out and do things is great. How do you pick? She has done so much."

by
Shirley A. SERVISS

Here Comes Trouble

A lively woman with short blond hair, sparkling blue eyes and a mischievous grin meets me at the door of the condo. I'm not quite sure who I expected Marlene Melnychuk to be, but it wasn't this vivacious person who deftly straps a brace on her crippled leg, ties her shoelaces with her one good hand, mounts her new silver scooter and heads for the door. Before I can even offer to help, she is off the machine, doorstop in hand, to prop the door open for her exit. She allows me to retrieve the doorstop and close the door and we head for the elevators.

"I'd rather go somewhere else to talk," she told me when I set up the appointment, and I gather, correctly, it's because of her roommate's presence. She shares the roomy, sunlit condo near a local mall with the owner's daughter. Support workers help with the shopping and cooking. Although it's a lovely living space, the relationship is strained and Marlene is hoping to move. "I want to live by myself," she says. "I have before."

In the meantime, a motorized scooter she acquired recently through the Cerebral Palsy Association and Easter Seals has given her a new measure of freedom. "It's a lifesaver," she says as we head towards a strip mall in search of a coffee shop. Prior to receiving the scooter she walked or rode in a manual wheelchair, but this gives her much more mobility. "I named it Skydawn," she tells me, explaining that its model name, Cobra, wasn't feminine enough. "My middle name is Dawn and I look at the sky when I ride," she laughs. "Not really." It's the first of many jokes.

She revs up to top-speed so we won't keep traffic waiting as we cross the street. Marlene is clearly enjoying the opportunity to put the pedal to the metal and I have to walk quickly to keep abreast. "I'm a daredevil," she says, and describes an adventure she had while visiting relatives in California. She convinced her cousin to go with her to Disneyland on the bus and try out the rides. Her favourite was the Space Mountain roller coaster. "We had to line up and as we got closer we saw all sorts of signs warning us not to go on the ride if you were pregnant, had a heart condition or were handicapped. My cousin tried to talk me out of it, but nothing was going to stop me. We were placed in the very front car and had a thrilling ride. So much for that handicapped warning!"

We've barely met, but I'm already aware that nothing seems to faze Marlene even though the encephalitis she contracted at two years of age resulted in a spastic left hand and a dragging left foot. Encephalitis is an infection of the central nervous system that affects the brain. It can be acquired from bites by infected insects or through contact with the saliva of an infected person or animal. Marlene and her older sister Wendi contracted the virus from a neighbour's dog. Wendi suffered no lasting damage but Marlene spent over three weeks in a coma, emerging alive, but having to relearn how to walk, talk and feed herself—this time with the use of only one side of her body.

Her handicap didn't prevent her from exercising her will. "When Mom would dress me in clothes I didn't want, I would manage to get them all off, one hand or not, and dress in my choice of clothes," she says. "Being stubborn can get you into trouble, but I think it's been a good thing in my life too."

Much of Marlene's childhood and adolescence was spent at the Glenrose Rehabilitation Hospital undergoing various therapies and surgeries. It became her playground. During nap time she decided to find out what would happen if she stuck her hair barrette into a nearby electrical outlet. "The barrette melted down and so did the nurses and that is how I got my curly hair!" she says. Another time she decided to go exploring in her wheelchair. "I saw a little ramp close to the auditorium and decided to try it out," she says. "It was OK, but when I went around the corner there was a really steep ramp waiting for me. Now that was a ride! I zoomed down it with my hair flying, barely stopping before hitting the brick wall at the bottom. I whipped around the corner again and by

George, there was another ramp that had a brick wall at the end. I took that one on too, and what a blast!" Wheeling around another corner she discovered she was in the cafeteria where a group of nurses from her unit were having lunch. "They were extremely upset with me and told me I was not allowed to do that again!"

"My nickname at the Glenrose is 'Trouble,'" she tells me, blue eyes open wide.

"I can't imagine why," I answer.

School was difficult, says Marlene. "First they put me in a classroom for handicapped people. Then they transferred me to the vocational program at L.Y. Cairns." Her time at L.Y. Cairns was positive. Marlene liked to draw and won the competition to redesign the school logo. She was also class president.

When she was twenty, Marlene volunteered in the playroom at the Glenrose. It turned into a paying job, organizing the playroom and reading to, or playing with, the kids. It was a position she held for seven years. While working there, Marlene came to appreciate her own parents. "There were parents who couldn't deal with their kids when they got sick, so the child would have to go to a care centre," she says. She is grateful her family never gave up on her and credits them for instilling an attitude of independence. "My parents helped me to learn to do things for myself. They'd tell me that if I couldn't do something, to try again. If I still couldn't, then to find another way to do it."

Marlene lived alone in an apartment while she was working at the Glenrose. Her job in pediatrics was followed by another long-term position as an aide to the nursing assistants and recreational therapists who worked with stroke patients. This was followed by a job with the pharmacy department, transporting pharmaceuticals to various hospital units.

"I learned a lot working at the Glenrose," she says, "particularly medical terminology."

An unhappy work situation led to Marlene's decision to go on stress leave for five months. Upon her return to work, she fell and broke her hand. Her neurologist said she could no longer work and Marlene has been on long-term disability since then.

"It was really hard to not be working anymore," she confesses. "I love to meet people and I had a lot of fun there." Her outgoing personality is in evidence as we wait for our drinks and she visits with the barista and a woman who comes over to admire her scooter.

Having a scooter has not only expanded Marlene's horizons, but has garnered her more respect. "When I'm in the Mall, people part for the scooter like Moses parted the Red Sea. I don't even get to honk!" she says.

She lived with her parents again for awhile after her job ended. One day, while home alone, Marlene fell downstairs, hit her head on the concrete basement floor, and suffered internal bleeding. "I spent another birthday in the hospital," she says ruefully. "I was in the Alec [Queen Alexandra Hospital] for over two weeks and back to the Glenrose for two weeks."

When she had recovered, Marlene registered in the Community Enrichment Program offered by MacEwan College at their City Centre Campus. The program provides students with the physical, emotional, social and financial skills they need to lead more independent, fulfilling and rewarding lives. Courses include communications, human sexuality, financial management, healthy lifestyles, assertion skills training and self advocacy. The program also includes a trial residency in an independent living suite at Sir Douglas Bader Towers near the University of Alberta. "I'd love to live there again," she says.

Marlene did well in the certificate program, graduating in June as valedictorian for the class. She plans to continue taking communications and computer courses.

"I'd like to speak to groups about encephalitis," she says. "I'd also like to go to schools and talk to kids with disabilities about how important it is to have a good attitude, to learn about what they have and how to deal with it." She has already participated in a program at the General Hospital in which she spoke to students considering medicine as a career. She was pleased with their response.

"This was just after lunch when I would be falling asleep, but I got them laughing and their eyes were open and they had lots of questions," she said. She is currently attending Toastmasters at King's College to improve her presentation skills. Listening to her describe her presentations, it's difficult to imagine there is much room for improvement.

Marlene is also in physical therapy twice a week to improve her mobility. "I'm a waitful person," she says. "I wait all the time. Wait. Wait. Wait. Half an hour. An hour and a half." She is describing her reliance on

DATS [Disabled Adult Transportation System] to transport her to her appointments. "If they had competition, they might improve their customer service," she says.

Marlene would like to advocate for people who have disabilities. She would start with Edmonton City Council. "I'd like to say 'Mr. Mayor, don't walk in my shoes, ride my scooter for a week and a half. Or get in a wheelchair and stay there long enough to understand what people have to deal with when they're handicapped.'"

Issues that concern her include the lack of independent living facilities, transportation options, job opportunities and accessibility. When asked about breaking down stereotypes she says, "I'm not a person to break anything!"

She admits that her disability could be a deterrent for some people, preventing them from getting to know her better. "They may feel they have to give more of themselves to help me," she says. "But hey, I have a scooter and I get to drive it!" She gives me a thumbs-up with her right hand. "The ones that look at me funny—I might have to run into them," she says, quickly adding that she's not serious.

The granddaughter of a "preacher," Marlene was raised in a Pentecostal church and attends church regularly. Her religious faith is strong and she believes it is the reason nothing gets her down for long. "I don't even think about negative things," she says. "I listen to Christian music and read Christian books and use Bible verses to help me deal with things."

Marlene's experience growing up in a loving, supportive, extended family has also helped to shape her outlook on life. "They like to take me out and do things with me," she says. "Their attitude to me is the best. There are no walls." As a result she makes friends easily. "I have friends through work, school, church, Toastmasters... I make friends anywhere that I go."

The advent of the Internet and Speed Dating have made it even easier for Marlene to meet people and to contemplate being in a closer relationship. "I would like to get married," she admits. She attends a Christian Speed Dating event at a Ukrainian community centre once a month where participants are grouped according to their ages. "I'd like to meet someone in an older age bracket," she jokes. "If I did that I'd call him a 'Sugar Daddy.'"

She also participates in an Internet Christian Dating Service and has been developing a relationship with someone who interests her. She hasn't told him about her disabilities. "I'd like a person to like me for who I am," she says. "I'd like him to come here and meet me first."

Besides getting married, Marlene would like to write her life story, to travel and speak about her life. She believes she has lots to offer. "I believe God wants me to be an advocate—a person speaking for people with disabilities and helping them deal with problems." While working at the Glenrose, she found that people often approached her on the units and in the hallways. "They came to me with their concerns and wanted to talk to me," she says.

It's not difficult to imagine how her friendly, open manner, her optimism and empathy would draw others to her.

Daredevil Marlene has a few other plans for her future. "I'd like to sky dive once without anybody knowing," she says, proceeding to tell me how much she enjoyed white water rafting once with one of her cousins. "I was like a queen," she says. "I sat in the middle of the raft with the guide wearing a helmet and a wet suit. I didn't even have to paddle! It was really neat!"

"I'd like to go white water rafting again and trail riding," she says. "I like to draw. I love to fly. I like to watch TV." Why am I not surprised to learn that her favourite program is *Survivor*?

"Actually, I like everything."

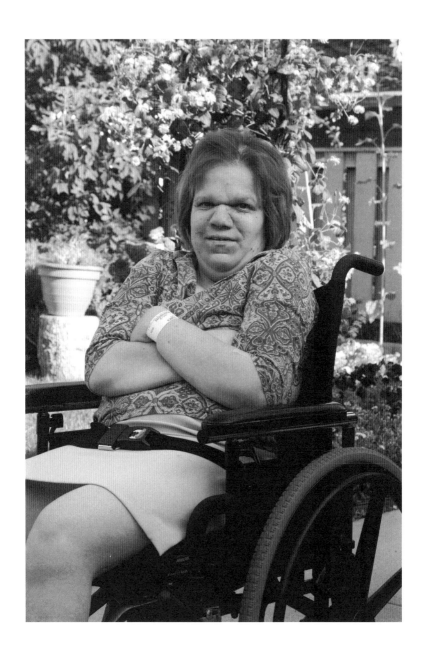

by
Debbie MARSHALL

Live Well, Laugh Much, Love Often

The doors of the darkened arena slide open and horse and rider are silhouetted in the bright autumn sunshine. Danita Schoenroth sits comfortably in the saddle, back straight, feet resting in the stirrups, relaxed hands holding the reins. In her down-filled coat and rubber boots, sandy brown hair tucked into her black riding helmet, she is well-prepared for the bitterly cold weather.

There are four other riders besides Danita. All are participants in the "Big Bits" program. Every Tuesday morning between May and November, adults with disabilities gather for an hour of riding at Edmonton's Whitemud Equestrian Centre. With the assistance of eager volunteers, they are helped onto the saddles of specially trained horses and accompanied as they ride down tree-lined paths.

Today Danita is riding a sturdy black quarter horse. As they amble along, a volunteer walks alongside and she and Danita carry on a spirited conversation. The volunteer does most of the talking, however, as Danita has limited verbal skills. This doesn't seem to bother her. She smiles, offers one-word answers, laughing whenever anything strikes her as funny. The conversation only stops when the riders are instructed to guide their horses into a circle or to the other side of the path.

The session ends back at the arena, where riders are invited to give their horses a final pat on the neck before they dismount. Danita needs only a little help to slip onto the portable steps that have been placed next to her horse. It is difficult to believe that this short, energetic 36-year-old was born with developmental and physical disabilities, along with heart and kidney problems. But the reality is that Danita spent the first five years of her life just struggling to survive. Only when doctors were finally able to get some of her ailments under control was she able to channel her energy into learning to crawl.

Today there is little evidence of that life and death struggle. Danita can walk short distances without assistance and enjoys swimming, dancing, and riding. She also loves to socialize. After her riding session, Jacquie Simmonds (the director of the home where Danita lives) asks her if she would like to go out for coffee.

"Party?" asks Danita with a crooked smile.

"Yes, we're going to have a kind of party," answers Jacquie. She explains that for Danita, everything is a party—from a coffee break to a Christmas open house. "Danita likes anything social," says Jacquie. "She's a free spirit who loves a party and asks for one all the time."

Our own "party" takes place at a Second Cup in a quiet suburban neighborhood. Danita orders an Italian soda while Jacquie and I sip hot coffee, shill shivering from our excursion at the Whitemud Centre. By comparison, Danita seems quite comfortable, busily drinking her cold soda while scanning the faces of the people in the café.

Although I initially try to direct my interview questions to Danita, it soon becomes clear that she isn't able to enter into a conversation or answer questions at length. Occasionally, she comes out with a complete sentence, but more often than not, she is only able to say a word or two. Jacquie therefore acts as her interpreter, answering questions and offering her own observations.

As Jacquie and I chat, Danita suddenly stands up and wanders over to the stand where jugs of milk and cream, and packages of sugar have been arranged for patrons. She is fascinated by a bald-headed man who has just sat down nearby to sip his coffee and read the newspaper. I envy her open curiousity. How many times have I been in a social setting where I have been afraid to introduce myself to an interesting looking stranger? With Danita, the barriers of social propriety are absent.

Jacquie coaxes Danita back to our table. "Danita is very observant. She notices when staff at the home change their hairstyles or wear new clothes," says Jacquie. She tells me that, on more than one occasion, Danita has surprised someone who she hasn't seen for years by remembering his or her name.

"Home?" Danita asks after taking her final sip of soda. "Home" is one of her favorite words. One of Danita's two homes is the Edmonton residence where she has lived for over 30 years. She is eager to return to that home today, since she and Jacquie are planning to decorate the house for their upcoming Christmas open house. I say goodbye and arrange to meet Danita a few days later.

It is a brisk, November morning when I arrive at the Edmonton home that Danita shares with four other people. Sunlight is pouring through a large bay window into the kitchen. Framed photographs of Danita and the other residents of the house are displayed on a sideboard against one wall. Two support workers are folding laundry at the large dining room table. I sit with Danita as she helps with the folding. Then she shows me her room. It is decorated in a warm country blue, with stuffed animals on the bed. The tops of her dresser and side table are overflowing with framed and unframed photographs of family and friends. I later learn that Danita spends many hours looking at old family photo albums and identifying the people in the pictures.

One photograph in Danita's collection catches my attention. It shows her dancing, wearing a pretty navy blue dress, a thin gold necklace, heavy black stockings, and sensible flat shoes. She holds her spastic hands in front of her, clapping to the music as she moves uncertainly across the floor. But there is no uncertainty about the kind of time she is having; she looks straight into the camera, a wide smile on her face.

Another figure is in the photograph; an able bodied woman who is also clapping and dancing. She is likely a support worker, ready to assist Danita as needed. When a person has a developmental disability, many of their relationships are with people who are paid to be with them. When those individuals leave for any reason, they feel bereft. Danita has built strong bonds of affection with staff and residents at the group home. This means that at times, she has had to endure painful losses. She goes through long periods of mourning whenever a staff member stops working with her. She seldom forgets their faces, and when she meets them again, she always remembers their names. Danita has also made close and enduring friendships with other residents at the Jasper Place home. Some of these friends have passed away and she has been left to grieve their loss.

Fortunately, family relationships have been more enduring. Once a month, Danita visits her parents Betty and Fred Schoenroth at their farm in Westerose, a small town southwest of Edmonton. Although her early health problems and the demands posed by her disabilities made it necessary for Danita to live in a supported living situation, her parents are careful to maintain her close connection to her family. According to Betty, "Danita loves everything out here and is happy to see me. 'My mum, my mum,' she always says. She is here at the farm for everybody's birthday and comes home for all the holidays—Christmas, Easter, and Thanksgiving."

"Danita knows a lot about love and knows how to share that love with others," says Betty. "She shows love by being attentive to others. She wants to be helpful; she tries to do anything she can for you. If she can just take laundry to the washer, then she's happy. She feels she's been helpful—that's important to her."

Danita loves riding on the skidoo with her father or spending time with her brothers Jeff and Kevin, sister-in-law Tammy, and her niece Taylor and nephew Ryan. "She's very entertained by the little ones," says Betty. "We've had a few family reunions at the farm. She sees aunts and uncles who she hasn't seen for years and she knows who they are."

Danita gets her love of horses from her connection to the farm. She spends most of her time outdoors, breathing in the scent of sweet hay and visiting the livestock and small animals that are part of farm life. "One of her favorite spots is the lawn swing," says Betty. "We have two cats who love to climb onto her knees."

Like most adults, Danita's life doesn't only revolve around fun family times. Although she is unable to hold a regular job, she volunteers once a week at a local daycare. Danita washes toys and spends time playing with the children. That work is important to her and a source of pride for her parents. Betty recalls attending a ceremony in which her daughter was given an award for her volunteer efforts. "It brought tears to my eyes," she recalls.

Danita is affectionate, blowing kisses to me when I visit. But while she has a soft and cuddly side, she also has a strong backbone. "If she wants something, she's not going to give in easily," says Betty Schoenroth. "And she'll certainly let you know if something is *not* what she wants."

Jacquie Simmonds agrees. She recalls the day when she took Danita out to buy protective headgear for her riding sessions. Many disabled riders are comfortable with bicycle helmets, but not Danita. "She insisted on a proper black riding helmet," says Jacquie. "So we took her out to the Tudor Tack shop and she got the helmet and boots—the whole deal."

There is a flip side to Danita's determination. She can be stubborn and intractable, lashing out when something doesn't go her way. On those occasions she lets others know she is unhappy, frequently telling them to "shut up." Like Danita, most people express their anger in disagreeable ways. However, Betty Schoenroth believes Danita's actions are also indicative of the challenges posed by her disability. "If I couldn't verbalize, I might strike out too…" she muses.

I would be disappointed if Danita didn't occasionally reveal a sense of fire and spirit. Determination, love of family, sense of home and relationships make her who she is. "Danita is a free spirit," says Jacquie Simmonds. Above her bed is a plaque with the words "Live Well, Laugh Much, Love Often." It seems an appropriate motto for a young woman, who despite daunting disabilities has made a life in which family and friends are central and for whom there is always time for a "party."

by
Gayle SIMONSON

Taming the Triggers

Swimming, horseback riding, dancing, rhythmic gymnastics—it is a schedule that would exhaust the average person. For Erin Kinloch-Galesloot, a busy community volunteer with many interests, it is her guide to healthy living. Erin has a genetic disorder known as Prader-Willi syndrome, a condition which leads to developmental delays but also to uncontrollable appetite. Without careful support, the condition can lead to morbid obesity and early death. Erin, with the support of family and caseworkers, has learned to resist food triggers—balancing a rigid diet and exercise program in order to gain some independence. She has completed a high school program, taken courses at MacEwan College, and now works part-time four days a week at PJ's Pets in West Edmonton Mall. Each step has taken hard work and determination, but according to Erin, her goal is to "gain more independence and achieve a better lifestyle."

One of the primary symptoms of Prader-Willi syndrome is an uncontrollable appetite by the time a child becomes a toddler. Parents of such children are confounded because, as babies, they had to be encouraged to eat and often failed to thrive. Muscle tone is poor and development is slow. Behaviour problems can develop as the child grows. Older children may be prone to temper tantrums, violent outbursts, and obsessive-compulsive behaviour. If they become morbidly obese, they may develop related health problems such as high blood pressure, heart disease and diabetes. Family support and understanding are required if these children are to develop healthy, active lives.

While today infants who fail to thrive are often identified at a young age, Erin wasn't diagnosed until age eight. Her mother Brenda Kinloch says that may have been helpful, since at that time, much of the literature surrounding the disorder focused on the negative and didn't offer much hope. However, once Erin was diagnosed, her parents faced many challenges in trying to help their daughter. Like most teenagers, Erin tended to rebel against the restrictions her parents placed on her. Brenda began to feel like the "Food Police," placing a lock on the fridge and constantly monitoring Erin's food intake.

Brenda credits current caseworker Marina for helping Erin on her road to success. Marina has worked with Erin for more than five years and that stability has been very positive. A change in diet and increased activity have led to a significant loss of weight. Those with Prader-Willi gain weight very easily on as little as 800 calories a day. For Erin, gaining control of her eating was essential. The widely-recommended "stoplight diet" didn't work for her. On that diet, "red" foods are forbidden. These include pizza, pop, fatty meats, sweets and many other foods with concentrated calories. "Orange" foods such as cereals, breads, potatoes, pasta and corn are severely limited. Most of the diet consists of "green" foods—non-starchy vegetables, fruits, fat-free dairy products and protein in the form of baked or broiled fish or skinless poultry.

The idea of an imposed diet and "forbidden" foods removes any sense of control from the individual. Marina feels that it is important that the people she supports feel some degree of control in their lives. She introduced Erin to a diet in which she could make some choices herself after meeting interim goals. With that motivation, Erin worked hard and the process was successful. Positive results were evident very quickly. Within two to three weeks, her mood and behaviour had improved. It took time, but Erin stuck with the strict regime and lost a lot of weight. She is now a petite blonde with a warm shy smile. Her weight gives no indication of the struggles she faces daily.

"You have to work hard," Erin agrees, but she proudly acknowledges that "it is worth it." Today, she can safely walk through a mall food court without yielding to her food triggers. With all her other interests, food is not the issue it once was. Now she is freer to participate in community events.

Erin began school like any other child at age five. However, after a couple of years, it was obvious she could not cope with the regular school curriculum. By grade three she was enrolled in Special Education classes near her home in Sherwood Park and was fortunate to continue in special programs. Erin completed high school in the Integrated Occupational Program (IOP), a program that has now been replaced in Alberta with Knowledge and Employability courses. She shyly admits that she was on the Honour Roll in grade ten, and in grade twelve won awards in English and Social Studies.

MacEwan College offered Erin more educational opportunities. Their College Connection program offers students with developmental disabilities the opportunity to experience college life by attending classes and participating to the extent that they are able. For Erin, those classes focused on child care. Staff members help students to maximize their involvement in college life so Erin found this to be a very positive experience.

Once she had finished with that program, Erin put those child care skills to work at Keheewin School in south Edmonton. She helped with the kindergarten class for five years. Food lessons and food preparation in the classroom posed special challenges for Erin. The staff was very supportive, but eventually her hours were cut. When Erin decided not to continue at the school, they showed their appreciation of her work by giving her a big farewell.

Fortunately, the College Connection offers alumni support. After Erin left Keheewin School, she was placed in a volunteer position at PJ's Pets in West Edmonton Mall. There she has learned to care for animals, "washing puppies and cleaning birds." She is given a token pay for her work. The job has led to a new interest in animals and she has tried to learn a little on her own as well.

With the support and encouragement of her parents, Erin left home at twenty to live in a group home. Today she shares an apartment in downtown Edmonton with another young woman. This is still a supported living situation, with a lock on the fridge. However, there is more freedom for both women. In her former group home, Erin hadn't been allowed to own pets. Now, she is the proud owner of two cats, an all-black named Licorice and a pretty little black and white one named Oreo. Marina believes the cats are good therapy. Erin simply loves the sense of responsibility she gets from looking after them herself.

The goal of this living situation is to make the women more independent and more responsible for themselves. Marina notes that it is important that they have input into decisions affecting them so that they have a sense of control over their lives. Teaching them to do things others of that age take for granted, such as making their own appointments, is a big step in achieving that goal. Each step results in an increase in self-esteem.

The physical activities in which Erin is involved have played a big part in her weight loss and also in the development of her self-esteem. They have helped develop muscle tone, which is a problem for people with Prader-Willi, and also helped improve her flexibility and balance. She swims three mornings a week. Her interest in animals has also led her to horseback riding. She participates each Tuesday in the therapeutic riding program offered at the Whitemud Stables in Edmonton.

Rhythmic gymnastics is also an important component of Erin's program. She participates through the Special Olympics organization and loves all the elements of that sport—hoops, balls, ribbons and rope. The Special Olympics has contributed a great deal to Erin's quality of life, but unfortunately there is a lack of understanding of Prader-Willi syndrome even at that level. Erin had hoped to compete in a provincial competition in Lethbridge. Unfortunately she was not allowed to have a full-time attendant and could not attend without one. Erin prefers not to dwell on the disappointment. For her mother Brenda, it was a symbol of the misunderstanding of the condition that is prevalent even among those who are working with young people with disabilities. Despite the gains Erin has made, she cannot even spend a weekend without someone nearby who fully comprehends the seriousness of the eating disorder.

Through Marina, Erin is learning Spanish and Latin dancing. Marina wanted to broaden the opportunities for some of the young people she has encountered in her work. Dancing could increase their muscle tone, flexibility, coordination and balance while giving them the chance to learn new skills and music appreciation. Marina had some experience in Spanish dance and decided to set up a class at Sacred Heart School. She now has six pupils and feels that the class cannot be any larger. Her daughter assists by working on stage with the group while Marina teaches and supervises. The group has performed at a number of community and fund-raising events. For Erin, the chance to perform is especially exciting because she loves to dress up in the colourful costumes. She appreciates that, by doing something she loves, she can entertain others and help out in the community.

Erin can now dress up in everyday life, too. When she was heavier, finding clothes to suit a young person was difficult. Since she has lost weight, shopping for a stylish new wardrobe has become an exciting process.

When she is not busy with her scheduled activities and work, Erin likes to relax at home or visit friends. She visits with her family each weekend and loves to play board games or watch movies with them. Romance and action movies are her favourites. Her extended family lives in the area, so gatherings with them are an important part of every special occasion. Her favourite television shows include "As the World Turns," "Gilmour Girls" and "Felicity." Of course, with her busy life, she isn't always home when they are aired so the VCR is important to help her keep up with her programs.

Erin likes to visit her best friend Jamie for supper or just to spend time together. When Jamie, who has Down syndrome, moved away from home, Erin was glad to be able to help by giving her some advice and helping her adjust to her new more independent lifestyle. Jamie's building has a swimming pool so the two can sometimes get a little unscheduled recreation and exercise!

What is next for Erin? Now that she has reached her goal weight, she is looking forward to a meal of vegetarian lasagna and a taste of real ice cream, something she has never had. However, her goals go far beyond food. When I met with her, she was eagerly looking forward to a rhythmic gymnastics competition to be held at the Alberta School for the Deaf. There, they would be "competing for real medals, not ribbons!" She also hopes that her Spanish dancing will progress to the stage where she can do real flamenco and dance the tango. She already has the shoes!

Erin would like to encourage others to learn more about Prader-Willi, "to check it out on the Internet or in the library so that there is more understanding of the condition in case they come across it." Others need an awareness that "a safe environment is essential until you get control."

What advice would Erin give to others with Prader-Willi? Her outlook is positive. "It is a challenge to work with but not impossible. Put your mind to it—you can do it!" Erin certainly has done it.

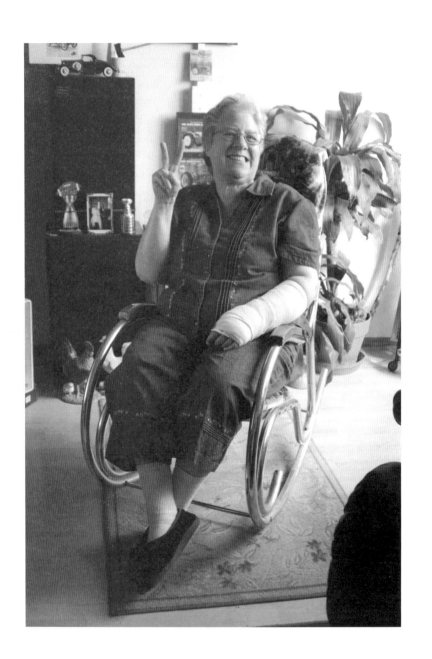

by
Sophie LEES

Tugboat Annie

Had I simply passed by Ann Tremblay on the street or sat next to her on a bus, I might have admired the smoothness of her skin, the agelessness of her face, or the soft blue-green-grey colour of her eyes. More than likely, these thoughts would have been fleeting—if I thought about her at all—because I would have seen an ordinary woman of average height and weight who reminded me of the grandmothers of my childhood friends. Indeed, the adjective that sticks in my mind is ordinary. Ann Tremblay looks ordinary. And, in many respects, she *is* ordinary—at age fifty-nine, she's been married for twenty-six years, owns a condo with her husband, and has worked fulltime for the Alberta government for thirty years—and that's what makes her so extraordinary. I wouldn't have known she has a developmental disability.

I meet Ann at the cozy home of her good friend and former co-worker, Carol Kucharski, who has known and been a staunch supporter of Ann since they first worked together in 1984. The first thing Ann does is hug me. She is known for her hugs. As Carol told me: "If she's having a bad day or thinks you're having a bad day and you need a hug, you'll get a hug." But at work, even more than her hugs, she's known for the nicknames that she applies to her friends.

"Carol's nickname is Shrimp," Ann announces, as we sit down. She informs me there was a time between 1985 and 1997 when she gave people nicknames and recorded these meticulously on a co-worker's computer.

By 1997, she'd accrued 150 names—a list of eight pages—before she'd had enough. "I ran out of names," she tells me. The people wanting names who came to her after that point were disappointed. Ann's own nickname is Tuggie, which derives from the movie character Tugboat Annie, who never let the odds get the best of her. It suits her perfectly.

Ann calls herself slow, and I suppose it's as good a word as any to describe her disability. Her balance is slightly off, causing her to be clumsy at times. She used a cane until three years ago when Carol pointed out she didn't really use it. "It was a security blanket," she says. Her speech impediment is more apparent than her clumsiness. Her pronunciation can make words hard to distinguish and when she's excited or trying to explain a complex situation or concept, she becomes frustrated. Sometimes she can't find the words she wants, but none of this can disguise the fact that Ann is a gifted storyteller with a wicked sense of humour. She also has an amazing ability to recall dates, which punctuate her stories.

This evening, Ann treats us to many stories about her life. She starts before she was born and says that she is the product of a romantic love-at-first-sight story. In that story, her father whistles at the sight of her mother's hair blowing in the breeze and her mother turns around to see the whistler, only to catch his eye and fall in love. Her parents were married on November 4, 1925, and for twenty-three years, they lived in Cardiff, Alberta, where Ann's father was born and raised. They had seven children: two boys and five girls. Ann, the youngest, was born on July 5, 1947. At age thirty-nine, her mother experienced a difficult pregnancy and labour. Ann's was a dry birth. Weighing four pounds, ten ounces, she was also a blue baby who quickly developed jaundice. By seven months, she had only gained five pounds. "My mom and dad said I looked like a little green monster from outer space," Ann quips. Her timing causes Carol and me to squeal with laughter at something, in retrospect, that doesn't seem so funny. But I imagine that Ann's humour is a gift that her family, the cornerstone of her strength, nurtured in her.

Growing up, Ann was very close to her sister Gail, who's just fourteen months older. "Gail took care of me," Ann says. "She talked to me." Ann didn't walk until she was three and didn't speak until she was eight, and even then, it took another seven years of struggling before she could make herself understood. She credits her parents who made her repeat her thoughts until the words were clear. Even though her speech can be somewhat hard to understand, Ann's desire to communicate in situations in which she feels comfortable is strong. And she says that she does the same thing with her husband Louie as her parents did with her. "He has the same habit as me now, repeating," she says. "I make him repeat and repeat. He gets so mad at me."

Ann's parents were determined that Ann would make it in the world as an independent person. "My parents never, ever let me give up from day one," Ann says. When she was little, they moved to Edmonton so that Ann could have the opportunities that a larger centre could offer, such as specialized education, rehabilitation, and job training. Still, it was hard work, with some tough parenting, at least on her mother's part. Ann describes her mother as an "iron fist." Her father, with whom Ann had a very close relationship, she calls a "marshmallow." "The last time I got really angry, both of them said, in the same voice, that they were doing it for my own good and that one day I would thank them for it," Ann recalls. "Guess what happened? I did!"

After eight years at the training centre, Ann was ready to pursue her independence. She started her job with the Alberta government on January 4, 1977, and a few months later, just shy of her thirtieth birthday, she moved into her own apartment. Now, three decades later, she still has the same job, which includes responsibilities such as shredding, photocopying, mail, deliveries and mail-outs. "I really like my job," she says. She's not like other people she sees who "want to pitch their computers out the window or kick them."

Ann doesn't live alone and hasn't for twenty-six years, not since she married Louie. Eager for another romantic story, I ask Ann if, like her mother, she fell in love at first sight. Ann answers with a hesitant "yes" and then tells us the story. In January 1978, she met Louie at an evening social at Rundle Park. Ann came with her girlfriend Heather, and she noticed Louie standing around. "He was doing nothing," Ann says. Louie came over and asked Ann's girlfriend to dance. Luckily, Ann recalls, "She said, 'Ask my friend.'" So Louie and Ann danced, but it was a disaster. "Then we tried to twist. I fell down. I went one way and my drink went the other," she pauses for comic effect. "Then we're dancing and I ask him, 'Are you French?' and he says, 'Yep,' and then, guess what happened? He started talking French to me!" Twenty-six years later, she claims she knows only twenty-four French words, mostly profanities. It took her three months to say *merci beaucoup* properly.

After their first meeting, Louie and Ann got to know each over the telephone for the first three months. During this time, the pair decided not to have children. Ann's mother supported this decision. In fact, she would agree to their marriage only if Ann underwent sterilization. Her father, a strong Catholic, wanted Ann to wait and decide for herself. Ann had the operation, but for many years kept it a secret from Louie's family, knowing that some believed the decision whether to have children is one only God should make. Thinking about her choice, Ann is a little wistful. "Sometimes, I wish…" she says, and then she laughs. " But then I hear other people's children." She makes the sound of a baby's cry and her wistfulness disappears.

Ann and Louie were married on April 12, 1980, three months after her father died from colon cancer. When Ann was first married, she found it hard to adjust. She missed her father terribly and subconsciously wished for Louie to be more a father figure than husband. Louie wasn't happy in this role and let Ann know it. This transition from daughter to wife, coupled with the grief of losing her father was the beginning of Ann's struggle with depression.

Her depression worsened when she started taking a new medication. Within three months, Ann lost a significant amount of weight, became increasingly paranoid and was wracked by dreams of her father asking her to join him in heaven. She thought of overdosing but knew she couldn't. Yet she couldn't talk about what was happening. "My parents told me if I wanted to make it in this world, I had to listen, watch, and zip it up," Ann says, miming a zipper closing over her lips. Finally, she was hospitalized on March 17, 1989. Even in the hospital, Ann remembers, "I have to keep everything inside." That is, until Carol came to visit.

When Carol saw Ann in hospital, Carol could see that she had "crawled into a shell," and so she told her, "Ann, if you need to cry, cry." Those were the magic words. "Well, she bawled and I bawled. And the nurses came running," Carol remembers. Their relationship blossomed from friendly co-workers to close friends.

But more than extending friendship, Carol cleaned up Ann and Louie's messy financial affairs. The couple were able to purchase a condominium in 1985. That's not all; when the mortgage was paid off in 2000, they renovated it completely. But at the beginning, turning their financial situation from red to black and teaching the couple how to manage and budget their money wasn't easy, Carol admits.

With Ann at work during banking hours, it seemed natural that Louie, who is unable to work, would take charge of the couple's finances. Unfortunately, much to the frustration of Ann's sister Gail and her new friend Carol, Louis didn't understand the need for budgeting. Instead, he would spend whatever was in their bank account, neither following their budget nor accounting for bills. After several financial crises, Carol gave him an ultimatum: either follow her budgets or she would get a trustee to look after their money. It took two years for the money mess to be sorted out. "It was a tough battle all around," Carol chuckles, "But something had to be done." Now the couple has banked some savings. They enjoy a weekly dinner out on Fridays and soon they'll enjoy going out on Sundays too.

As our evening unfolds, Ann wonders how Louie is doing—he stayed home so that we women could talk more freely. Both Carol and Ann agree that he's probably pacing the living room floor. Louie doesn't like to be away from Ann. They are, as Carol puts it, "inseparable." He takes the bus to work with Ann in the morning and meets her after work so they can ride the bus home together. If she has a doctor's appointment, he'll come too. They've had their ups and downs like any couple, but they're still going strong after twenty-six years.

Perhaps the secret to their marital success is that Ann—like her namesake Tugboat Annie—has managed to maintain her own identity. An incident that happened ten years ago perfectly illustrates her ability to do what she thinks best, even when her partner disagrees. Ann and Louie usually went to visit his family for a few weeks each year. But in 1997, Ann's mother suffered her fourth heart attack and entered the hospital for the last time. Ann recalls, "I told Louie, 'This not the time for me to go up north with you, you have to go up by yourself.' He wouldn't take no for an answer, but I said, 'If anything happens to my mom, forget it, I'll feel too bad.'"

That week, Louie went up north and Ann saw her mother every day. She remembers that she had one picture left on the film in her camera. She asked a friend to take a picture of Ann and her mother. Ann, an avid photographer, tells me she took pictures from 1973-1997. She has twenty-three albums of photographs. I wonder if this photo—the one of Ann and her mother—was the last photo Ann developed, but I don't ask. Instead, Ann shares a remarkable insight. "My mom was a good person, but she was scared of being hurt," Ann tells us, "So she put a shell all around her so she wouldn't get hurt. She was twelve years old when her mom passed away."

Ann still has to deal with her own shell, her continuing struggle with depression. Life, as we know, isn't easy, and it's always throwing some challenge or another at us. "With Ann, things really get to her," Carol observes. "And then she starts going down, and you can actually see it happening." It's hard for Ann to express those negative feelings. As Carol says, "Her biggest fear is getting in trouble, people yelling at her."

I notice that Ann looks a little sad when I enthuse about her accomplishments, as though she might feel guilty for ever having a negative thought, for not being wholly grateful for the support she's received or proud of achieving normalcy. And I just want to hug her, not for her exceptional achievements, but for her humanity, her humour, her generosity, her indomitable spirit. Tugboat Annie.

by
Christie SCHULTZ

At Twenty-Seven:
Dean Kirkby's Story

With only his photo album in front of us, it would be easy to assume that Dean Kirkby's childhood was a lot like mine. His mother Lori is turning the pages and they are both pointing out the best photos. They smile as they revisit the pictures of best friends playing together or Dean with his favourite teacher. We pause to admire the photo of Dean posing in a new outfit for a childhood dance recital. I tell Lori that these remind me of the photos in my mom's albums from when I, too, was an excited six-year-old in a new dance costume.

"I was really nervous," retired dance teacher Joan Ward admits. Dean Kirkby was the first child with Down syndrome that she had taught.

"Lori thought Dean should have dance lessons like his older sister and I really worried about it at first," she tells me. "I thought, 'What am I going to do with Dean?' and then, looking at the class, I thought, 'I'm going to treat him like everybody else,' and it worked."

Joan explains that this meant that everyone understood that there were things that Dean could and couldn't do. But it also meant that he was included with other children his age. Together, the children learned to take instruction and stand at the ballet barre or in a straight line. They memorized dance steps. That was more than twenty years ago.

The night I first meet Dean, he is watching *The Fifth Element*, one of the two videos he has chosen for the evening. The enthusiastic and protective greeting of four barking dogs emphasizes my interruption.

I've made my way from Edmonton to Stony Plain, face first into the late-March sunset. When I arrive, Dean doesn't allow my arrival to distract too much from the movie. His couch is only a few feet from the front door though, so with prompting from his mother, he offers a "Hi." When Lori asks him to get up and say hello, he says "Come on, Mom," and gestures to the screen. It's clear that he wants to watch the end of the movie before he takes time to talk with me.

But I feel welcomed into their home. I'm offered a seat on the other couch in their bright blue living room and take a few seconds to remember the plot of *The Fifth Element*. A pair of budgies chirp and mutter to each other as I settle in.

The dogs head out to the yard and while Dean is watching the last few minutes of the movie, Lori introduces a few other members of the family who have made their way into the living room. Arleen is the eldest of Lori's four children and the mother of two children in the room, Brieann and Kyle. At ages six and eight, the grandchildren are a flurry of play, stopping only to interject when they have something to add to the conversation. We have a few minutes to chat while Bruce Willis figures out how to save the world.

"The first thing you need to know about Dean is that he loves movies," Lori says. "He works in two video stores during the week."

The movie collection that surrounds the television is vast, stacked on both sides and across an entire shelf below. A few cases sit on top of the television, but it looks like a well-organized collection. When I comment that there are a lot of movies, Brieann tells me that there are even more in the basement. She adds, "Today, we get to watch *The Cat in the Hat*," the other film Dean has borrowed for tonight.

"Dean is really great with the kids," says Lori. Their mom, Arleen, agrees. Dean looks over with an "Aw, Mom" at this or whenever she reveals something endearing or sentimental. His reaction to his mother's pride is what I'd expect from anyone our age. Born in the late seventies, both Dean and I are twenty-seven.

When Dean started grade one, he got on a yellow bus and left his neighbourhood to attend a school that offered a segregated classroom for children with special needs. Lori tells me that the experience severely limited his interaction with children in his community. Responding to this, the Kirkby family participated in an integration pilot project set up by Stony Plain's Forest Green School and the Country of Parkland Central Administration staff. Dean was the first child in the County of Parkland with a developmental disability to be fully included in a classroom with so-called normal children.

The learning curve for staff at Forest Green School was steep. Lori shares with me a letter written by his grade five teacher, Lawrence Cooper. He acknowledges that Dean's presence in the classroom taught students a great deal about tolerance and compassion.

"Through regular meetings with his friends, we expanded their knowledge and skills so that Dean was accepted and included in every facet of his program," he wrote. "We learned to accommodate his inability to catch a basketball, his inability to read in Language Arts projects, and his tendency to fatigue and tire in his classroom activities and group projects. With the help of his friends, Dean became accepted and appreciated in every activity of the day."

In the letter, Lawrence notes that he had to throw out some of the planning and organizing methods with which he was familiar, but that "Strategies that work well for integration are just plain good teaching strategies. They benefit all kids."

Janet South, Dean's academic aide throughout grades five, six, and the first part of grade seven, says that her experience working with Dean taught her a great deal. For example, "Telling time is a difficult concept for most children and it was especially difficult for Dean. It took some work, but I realized that I needed to use stronger visual aids for Dean," she says. "Eventually, we learned to write the schedule on the board, often with pictures, and erase what we had finished so that Dean could see how much time was left in the day." Little things like this helped Dean and helped Janet to "learn new ways to teach any child."

While Janet doesn't ignore the fact that there were bullies in the school, she notes that the "circle of friends" groups they established for all the students really helped them learn to support each other. When bullies appeared, Dean had a circle of friends nearby. In fact, Dean's school friends get the credit for saving him from the neighbourhood bullies who once tied ropes around Dean's neck and then got ready to ride away on bikes. Just in time, the circle of friends told the bullies to leave Dean alone.

In this context, the photos of Dean smiling and playing with his friends stand out more than just casual snapshots: without the integration pilot project, Dean might not have had the opportunity to share a classroom, friendships and photos with neighbourhood kids. And, while the contents of the photo album resemble those found in many family collections, there is also an addition. Tucked inside is a copy of a letter written by Lori to the principal of the local high school. It reads: "We would like Dean to be fully included into Grade 10 at Memorial Composite High school, appropriately supported, as required. We would like Dean to have opportunities for normative experiences where friendships are supported and facilitated. We expect Dean's educational goals to be based on the same curriculum as the other students but to be modified and adapted to meet Dean's individual, educational requirements. We do not expect Dean to be brought up to grade level. Communication, social interactions, literacy and computer skills are priorities for our family."

The letter—along with the efforts of family, teachers and aides—worked. Dean continued in an integrated classroom for the rest of his schooling.

As *The Fifth Element* finishes, Dean reminds his mom that it was almost at the end when I arrived. "See, Mom," he teases. Communicating is often difficult for Dean, but it's clear that he wants to engage with us now that the movie is finished. Lori asks Dean to name his favourite movie and he picks out *Hulk* from the shelf. As if on cue, his younger brother Dale, twenty-four, joins us in the living room and reveals, "That's the only movie Dean ever takes from my room." Dale seems quiet and reserved, but I quickly get the impression that he is one of his brother's staunch defenders. In the past, his older sister, Arleen, also played that role, sometimes to the point of getting reprimanded for coming to Dean's rescue. "I'd defend him if I had to, even if I got into trouble for it," she tells me. "But we also helped Dean to learn to take care of himself."

After graduating from high school, both Dale and Arleen worked in jobs helping other adults with disabilities. "I saw how my brother was treated sometimes," says Arleen, "And I wanted to help others to be treated better." Arleen's story is cut short as Dean starts to share more about his favourite movies. He picks out a few more to show me, including one of my personal favourites, *Back to the Future.*

Arleen invites the dogs back in house and Scruffy, the smallest of the four dogs, sidles up to me and becomes a new furry friend. Scruffy is Dean's dog, Lori tells me, and I feel honoured to share Scruffy's affection.

Kim, the youngest of Dean's siblings at seventeen, joins us as well. She flops down onto the couch where Dean is sitting, putting her arm around him. With so many people in his family, I ask Dean if he still has time for friends.

"Daveen, friend," Dean says. Daveen Little is the aide who works with Dean during the week.

Lori explains that a lot of Dean's other friends have moved away recently and that she struggles to help him make new friends. "The people he works with are more like his friends," she says.

That's not so uncommon, I think. In the past year, five of my own friends have moved away, either for school or work or both. Having chosen to stay in Edmonton, I am also experiencing the difficulty of developing new friendships and have begun to forge new friendships with co-workers. It strikes me that a lot of people who don't move away from home in their late twenties have this experience in common.

We share this, Dean and I, one of the struggles of being twenty-seven.

Dean invites me to join him during his shift at Movie World so that I can better understand what he does on a daily basis. I arrive ahead of time and scan the shelves: alphabetically arranged new releases on the outer walls, older titles on the central stacks. It's like every other video store except that, before I browse through half the alphabet, Dean arrives with Daveen and welcomes me with a warm "Hi." Almost before I can return the greeting, he gets to work, taking videos and DVDs out of the return drop box and stacking them neatly so that they can be scanned back into the system. Once the items have been scanned, he puts locks on movie cases and Daveen helps to alphabetize the pile. The store often rents five hundred items per day, so this is no small task. After about thirty minutes of stacking, scanning, locking and sorting, Dean is ready to start putting the movies back on the shelf.

We move through the store, re-filling the shelves with "viewing pleasure." Dean is familiar with the process and often finds the correct spot for the movie before I see it.

"He was even better at this before he got sick," Daveen tells me. "But I think that his illness really affected his literacy skills."

In early 2001, Dean almost died due to complications from a lung infection brought on after choking on a hot dog. He spent weeks in hospital and months recovering at home. Both Daveen and Lori feel certain that the experience affected more than his body. But he's healthy now, and he's happy to be back at work.

When we talk about Dean's love of movies, Lori confesses that she used to worry that Dean watched too much television and too many films.

"A lot of parents of children with disabilities are criticized for letting their kids watch too much TV," she says. "But I've watched Dean respond to movies in the same way I respond to books. He's really engaged when he's watching a movie."

From his response to *The Fifth Element*, I have no doubt that she's right and that Dean has found his passion—a passion that he expresses both at work and at home. Before he leaves for lunch, Dean chooses the movies that he'll watch in the evening. He takes me through the aisles at the store, pointing out movies he likes. The first movie he chooses today is *Harry and the Hendersons*, another of his favourites and one that he will enjoy with his niece and nephew.

Before I go, I ask Dean how he feels when he has trouble communicating. He says to me, *"You know."* It's a response that he offered occasionally during our visits when he didn't quite have the words. But as an answer to this question, it's exactly right. I do know what it's like. Finding words is one of the hardest things I do.

There are differences between Dean and I, but our similarities stand out more than I would have anticipated. Like Dean, I attended children's dance lessons where I awkwardly learned routines and enjoyed the click of tap shoes. Today, like him, I struggle to figure out how to be twenty-seven. And when I attend a writing class the day after meeting Dean, I think about him as we all search for words.

by
Kalin JENSEN

My Ears, Joe's Tongue, Ryan's Finger, Jackie's Throat, Erik's Heart

The room is small. Dark cases clutter the space as a handful of eighth graders take their places for rehearsal. The flutists giggle and the percussionists examine their wooden mallets. Christian Bayus, a blond 15-year-old in an Oilers' jersey, raises his clarinet to his lips. The teacher, holding a trumpet at the front of the class, raises his finger to cue the band as the woman sitting next to Christian taps hers on his sheet music. The band begins the *Colonial March*. With each note, the woman glides her finger across the bars of music. When a trombonist pretends to conduct between slides of his trombone, Christian becomes distracted and begins to fall behind. The woman next to him taps his sheet music emphatically. Christian moves closer and closer to the music stand in concentration. His notes slowly catch up to the other musicians. When the piece ends, the band teacher looks over to his section and remarks, "Nice job, clarinets."

I watch a video of the concert on a laptop with Christian's mother. His blond hair is hardly visible in the film, but the sound from his clarinet is sharp and clear. With only one missed note, the solo is nearly perfect. Karen Pedersen-Bayus' eyes smile proudly as she watches her son bow at the waist to the sound of applause streaming through the speakers. "I enrolled Christian in a music program for toddlers when he was two. I did the same thing with his older brother and sister, but it didn't stick with them." His mother looks over at me with the sparkle still lingering in her eye. "But with Christian, it did."

Christian is one of five students at Richard S. Fowler Junior High with Down syndrome. Most of these teenagers are secluded together for most of the day, joining the rest of the students only during options. However, with the exception of Language Arts and Math, Christian always attends class with his grade nine peers. At times, the curriculum is adapted for him to accommodate his proficiency level. When other students learn about the chemical reactions in the stomach, Christian learns where the stomach is located. His mother hopes he will continue to be integrated into regular classes throughout high school so he can continue to socialize with other students his own age.

Mary Watkinson is Christian's private music tutor. At the age of seven she taught him to play the xylophone. He learned to read notes and began to play the soprano recorder at nine. Three years later Christian added the alto recorder to his repertoire and later, the tenor recorder and clarinet. He plays the recorders in the student concerts that Mary organizes, while he plays the clarinet mainly in the school band. Mary has Christian play a variety of instruments in any given lesson in order to keep him fresh for performances.

The majority of Mary's students are not developmentally disabled. However, she does have a few students—including Christian—that require additional attention. "For every step I take with a regular child, I break into four for Christian," she explains. He helps bridge this gap by practicing at home alone in the afternoon and with his mother in the evening. This is all done between school, his chores—dishes, laundry, sorting recycling—his friends, and spending time with his family.

Christian shows up at his private lesson in blue slacks, a white shirt, and a Christmas tie: red, with little white igloos. The skinny tail of the tie continues for a good six inches too long. He sits on a chair in front of me and opens his backpack, eying me curiously. Mary rushes over and loops the long-end through the band behind his tie, murmuring something about a tie clip. During this primping session, Christian drops his backpack and looks alternatively between Mary's hands and myself. After finishing, Mary continues our conversation about Christian and music. He follows our conversation with his eyes. I find it awkward to talk about him as if he wasn't there. I turn to Christian and ask him if he likes playing in the band.

138

He pulls the long end of his tie back through the band to let it hang free. "Yeah," he nods, "I like it a lot."

Christian's mother Karen is also attending the lesson today. She began working as a Learning Support Consultant for Greater St. Albert Catholic Schools before Christian was born. As a result of the skills she learned as a consultant, she was better prepared than most new mothers for raising a child with Down syndrome. When her son was still very young, she taught him sign language in order to facilitate communication. Although he relies almost exclusively on verbal speech, at times he falls back on finger-spelling to get his message across. Karen took only two months off for maternity leave and discovered that Christian was "very much like a typical baby. He did not take more time or more care." However, for the first five years of his life, he got sick more often than his brother or sister, spending roughly one week per year in hospital.

Fortunately, once he began elementary school, Christian's immune system kicked in. He was rarely sick, but now needed a different kind of attention. Christian was quickly falling behind with reading and other comprehension skills. By the time he reached junior high, an aide would attend classes with him, providing him with the one-on-one attention that he needed. Christian was no longer assigned homework, since Karen found that he was not capable of working at the same level and pace as many of his peers. Practicing the clarinet and recorder now occupied much of his free time.

Music is now a central focus in Christian's life. At his private music lesson, he prepares two recorder pieces—one solo and one ensemble— for a concert next month. His mother points a small camcorder in his direction, its red recording light flashing. Christian does well in the beginning, but falters whenever his recorder attempts a D-note. After Mary tells him to press harder on the note to fully seal the hole, Christian takes a deep breath and tries again. His face tenses in anticipation. At the crucial moment, his lip curls tightly and his fingers clench hard as a perfect note spills out.

Christian takes the seat across from me as Mary finds the next accompaniment tape. Karen places the camcorder on her lap. "I want to show the high school band teacher what he's capable of. What his level is at." she explains. When Christian first decided he wanted to play in the school band, neither Karen nor Mary could determine his playing level. He had been playing the recorder for years but never in a class full of students playing many different instruments, each entering in the music at so many different places. The women thought he would probably be placed with the seventh grade band, and were surprised when the band teacher felt he would fit in with students nearer his own grade. Although Christian played a fraction of the number of pieces that the rest of the band did, he found great satisfaction in playing with his peers. Karen hopes that he will be allowed to continue to participate with his band-mates when he enters high school.

Throughout his music lesson, Karen keeps her camera on Christian when he does well and does not remove it when he falters. Also recorded are Mary's instructions and Christian's attempted corrections. I wonder if it is hard to fight the urge to edit out the shaky parts and only show the best. Mary signals that she is ready for Christian to continue with rehearsal. Grabbing his alto recorder, he turns to Karen and asks, "Hey Mum? You gonna tape me?" His mother laughs and raises the camera back into the upright position.

Later, sitting around the kitchen table at the Bayus home, I ask Christian to describe what it's like to have Down syndrome. Without hesitating, he responds, "My ears, Joe's tongue, Ryan's finger, Jackie's throat, Eric's heart." His mother explains that Christian picks out other people who have the syndrome by identifying some of their physical characteristics (even if these qualities have nothing to do with the syndrome). His friend Ryan must prick his finger because he has diabetes. Another friend, Joe, had a swollen tongue during a bout of tonsillitis. And Christian himself is almost entirely deaf in one ear.

When asked if people treat him differently because he has the syndrome, Christian responds: "Yes. For good." He continues to talk, but his words become muddled. His mother tells him to try again. Carefully enunciating, he continues, "I listen to them. I talk slow. Not too fast."

"There is still a bell curve of ability at play in people with Down syndrome," Karen explains as Christian checks hockey stats online in the other room. "Christian does quite well, but other kids need more help." She speculates that it helps that Christian is the youngest of three children. He has older siblings to look up to and strive to match. This is another reason why Karen hopes Christian will be allowed to stay in regular classes throughout high school. Although his ability is lower than average, he has more to aspire to in a room full of typical children, than in a setting with those who are developmentally disabled.

A family's attitude is also a critical factor in the success of a child with Down syndrome, just as it is with any child. There is a delicate balance between giving the extra care and attention needed and over-protecting a child. This school year, Christian will learn how to take public transportation by himself to school and back. Karen admits that she and her husband are somewhat frightened at the prospect of letting their son loose in the big bad world. In the end, however, they know he's capable of the added responsibility.

When I ask Christian if there's anything he feels he cannot do because he has Down syndrome, he had only two answers: driving and college. His mother quickly leaps in and tells him that he can go to NAIT when he finishes high school. In fact, Christian frequently talks about going to college and may be entering the point in his life in which the natural insecurities of adolescence make him doubt his capabilities. On the issue of driving, however, his mother confirms that this is one skill that Christian will never learn. She debated whether or not to prolong the denial by telling him he could learn when he was older, but decided it was best to let him know straight out that people with Down syndrome cannot drive. This is hard for Christian and a source of frustration, since most of his peers are obtaining their permits and testing their parents' vehicles on the road. By navigating public transportation, Christian will gain a means of mobility but not in the same way as his friends. He is able to overcome many obstacles through concentration and practice. He has conquered recorders, the clarinet, and the dreaded D-note, but in this one instance his will to overcome is not enough.

I think back to the first time I met Christian—at a band practice. I had arrived early. Christian's teacher and I were alone in the room. He was gathering the music for the day. I was sitting in a small chair at the back of the room. I asked the teacher what he thought of Christian. He looked over at me and explained that Christian was just like any other junior high student, "a really good kid most of the time" but sometimes frustrating and challenging. Then the teacher paused. "It's not his fault. He's fifteen, after all."

by
Allan CHAMBERS

Launching into Life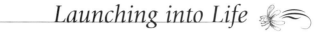

There is something profoundly comforting about a transit bus. It has its known schedules, its specified times of arrival and departure. It won't surprise you by suddenly veering into the unknown. As a means of travel, it is safe and reassuring, especially when drops of summer rain are trailing down the side windows or when snowflakes come swirling out of the darkness on a winter night. It is companionable, particularly if you are shy but want to be among people. It might even be the perfect vehicle for life's journey—just ask Blaze Logan.

He was hooked from the start. As a child, Blaze would arrive home from a bus trip and immediately sit down to capture the experience in a drawing. He had difficulty saying what he had seen, but he could create a picture that was almost photographic. Most kids draw a rectangle on two wheels. Blaze had detail. His buses were exact renditions, with a head in every window. His LRT drawings included not only the bridge across the river, but the passengers inside the cars, gazing out at the valley below.

Blaze would also go for rides with his older sister Rheanna, and the thrill never left. He committed routes and times to memory. Once he had done a route, he never forgot it. He became a traveling compendium of bus schedules. The world was opening up. After a while, he wanted to travel on his own.

Debbie Coulter, his mother, remembers that time clearly. Blaze was twelve or so and the family lived in Edmonton. "Bus adventures" were by then a big part of his life. Northgate was his launching pad—to

143

Castledowns, West Edmonton, and Mill Woods, anywhere a bus might take an observant boy with wide eyes and a trusting heart.

"He wanted to ride the bus on his own," Debbie recalls. "I was kind of scared. I also realized he needed to know how to get around the city. The skill required to get from Point A to Point B was more important to his life than my fear."

In his teenage years, Blaze shot upwards and outwards. He became big and strong. The year he turned seventeen, he went with his family to the annual Metis gathering at Batoche, Saskatchewan. Blaze entered the heavy-sack carrying competition, a game that harkens back to the days when Metis trappers and traders hoisted heavy bales of fur on their backs. Blaze won a silver medal.

"I had a load on me like this," he says, gesturing above his head as we stand in the basement of the northeast Edmonton bungalow he shares with his uncle, Cliff Coulter. "I had one guy on each side of me, watching me walk. I carried this load a couple of kilometres. Whoo!" He drops his arms and his face breaks into a wide grin. He is twenty-five now and he is strapping. His head, framed by a shock of black hair, nearly touches the low ceiling. His eyes are dark and friendly. His mother says that people never forget Blaze. Those who get to know him will frequently drop back into his life. They like him.

Riding the transit buses, Blaze got to know Edmonton well. He was the big kid in the back seats, noticing every rider who got on or off, checking out the passing neighbourhoods, music spilling out of his headphones—Ace of Base, Depeche Mode, Limpbizkit, Beastie Boys, Philosopher Kings.

"I like to see the neighbourhoods and the houses," he says. "I like to explore the industrial areas." When he has time to prepare his thoughts, he speaks with clarity and intelligence, only his twitching thumbs betraying his unease. "I sit near the back of the bus," he says. "I listen to my Walkman." He rattles off his musical preferences. "Rock, pop, retro, all sorts of music, groove music."

Debbie Coulter recounts Blaze's bus adventures, while he follows her descriptions closely. Her pride burns through. You can tell they have learned a lot from each other. "It helped him to move into a more independent adult feeling of taking care of himself, of knowing who he was and where he was," she says. "He is a great guy and he enjoys life. I didn't want to hinder that. I wanted to support his independence."

She laughs at how successful the bus adventures turned out to be. "He's memorized Edmonton," she says. "He names neighbourhoods and streets that I've never heard of. Now he has discovered that buses go to Calgary."

When Blaze was four, workers at his daycare told his mother that he didn't seem to be developing normally. Tests suggested development delays and autistic tendencies. It was a sobering diagnosis. Autism is a bewildering neurological disorder that can lead to profound behavioural and communication problems. Blaze might reach a developmental age of eight, Coulter was told. She refused to accept the prognosis.

Coulter is a single mother of four children, and she is a fighter. She comes by it honestly. Her own mother is Thelma Chalifoux, a single mother of seven children who became Canada's first Metis woman to be appointed to the Senate. Chalifoux retired from the Senate in 2004 and returned to her beloved cabin near Morinville, after earning a national reputation as an activist for Metis people and society's poor. Blaze, one of Chalifoux's thirty grandchildren, inherited her independent spirit and down-to-earth approach. So did Debbie Coulter. She knew she had a lot to work with.

Special education programs were taken up. Social agencies were enlisted. With tremendous family support and helpful agencies, Blaze graduated from L.Y. Cairns High School and entered programs that might lead to work. He took jobs as a cook in a restaurant and as a sweeper at the St. Vincent de Paul store. The aim was an independent life—or at least as much independence as Blaze could manage.

Coulter saw in Blaze the gifts he had brought to their family. In the past, they had moved around a lot, from Calgary to Medicine Hat, Slave Lake to Edmonton. When Blaze's developmental challenges were diagnosed, his mother was told that he needed regular routines and certainty in his life. Coulter and her children settled into a neighbourhood in northeast Edmonton and stayed. The stability benefited Blaze. It also helped his siblings, who developed routines and work habits that led them into productive university and work lives. There were other gifts too, and Coulter recites them with pride. "He finds it difficult to lie. That helps us all. His patience, his kindness, his honesty, his unconditional love…"

None of the available social programs had an aboriginal framework or cultural sensitivity. Blaze's family went to work. When he was ready to leave home in his early 20s, he moved in with Coulter's brother, Cliff, in a modest house owned by Thelma Chalifoux in northeast Edmonton. Cliff is disabled by a lung condition. Blaze is strong enough to help him with chores that Cliff can no longer do. Cliff, in return, works to turn Blaze's social weaknesses into strengths. For example, he will "talk through" social visits with Blaze before there is a knock on the door.

Elders were consulted and agreed: this matching of strengths and weaknesses, of Cliff's counsel and Blaze's physical strength, fitted with their traditional teachings.

"I help Cliff by taking out the garbage, shoveling the sidewalks," Blaze says. "Cliff lets me pay some of the bills. I help him make supper."

Together they make the rent, and a life. One winter, retired Senator Chalifoux stayed with them, but she missed her cabin. "She likes her coyotes and her hawks," Cliff says. Blaze nods understandingly. He is close to his grandmother, but he also knows her independent spirit. It is something he shares with her.

It is a long commute by transit from Blaze's home in northeast Edmonton to the industrial reaches of the southeast. You catch the No. 153 eastbound on 132nd Avenue and that gets you to the Belvedere LRT station. Take the train downtown and race over to the Telus stop for the No. 8 southbound. Ride it to the corner of 83rd Street and 82nd Avenue and then catch the No. 306.

That will take you most of the way, but you will still have to walk past chain-link fences lined with weeds, past exposed steel girders, concrete structures and abandoned couches, to get to the imposing CF Rotex materials-recycling plant.

Inside the plant, you will find the largest gathering of discarded garments you can imagine. It looks like a collection point for clothing destined for shipment to destitute countries. In fact, the garments are too far gone to qualify for donation. Instead, they will be transformed into cleaning rags for big industries like the oil, road machinery, and heavy equipment companies. Environmentally, it verges on a miracle. Think of all the ragged, worn-out sweats ever donned by the people of Edmonton. Now think of them recycled into a new useful product—that's what CF Rotex does.

Look skyward in the huge building and you can pick out human figures in the garment mountains. Working in teams of two, they're cutting clothing into sizes suitable for rags. Bins are filled and moved by forklift across the factory floor to the baler, a complex machine that measures, cleans and bags the rags. That might normally require two operators. Blaze runs it on his own, swiftly and skillfully.

He recently composed a story, printed with great care, in which he described his work. "The work I do there is baling up clothes rags through a baling machine, and stacking them on a pallet. And I make boxes and I do up garbage and I sweep up. It's like a warehouse and I've been taking the ETS buses there."

The baling machine requires concentration and adept movement, and Blaze operates it masterfully. In seconds, he packs armloads of garment pieces into the baling apparatus for compressing and cleaning, attaches a plastic bag to a chute, slaps in a label, catches the bag when it fills with twenty pounds of gaily-coloured rags, tapes the bag, stacks it neatly on a pallet and grabs another armload of remnants to begin the process again.

The company took a chance on Blaze, hiring him in a work experience project. They haven't regretted the decision. "He's fast," says Russell, the forklift operator and Blaze's supervisor, as the bright bales of discarded t-shirts and sweats pile up on the pallet. "If you had two people on that machine, it would just slow him down. He's an excellent worker."

At quitting time, the transit journey spools out in reverse. It takes an hour and a half to get home. Blaze doesn't mind. His workday is done. He's got his headphones. Every bus trip is a picture. Some of the drivers know him and say hello. He knows other people on the buses too because he sees them frequently. He is making his way. Recently, his mother says, an agency called to say he might qualify for another outreach worker. Blaze declined the offer. "He said, 'No, I'm a grown man now. I don't need any more workers.'"

When he gets home, Cliff will have a meal on. They might watch Sabrina the Teenage Witch or Lizzie McGuire, unless Cliff's Blue Jays are playing. If it is a hot evening, they might barbecue. There will be visitors. Blaze is slowly getting used to that, with Cliff's help. Bit by bit, surprise is entering his life.

It's a viable Edmonton life, nourished by family and supported by community. Ask him about his favourite place in Edmonton after all his bus travels and Blaze will respond that it is his mother's house. It is a few blocks away. Even so, he has traveled a long way from it, farther than might have been expected, and his journey is still in its early days.

by
Heather BOYD

An Irrepressible Imp

Carol Ann pulls up the T-shirt with the word "Barbados" emblazoned on the front and pushes the top of her pyjama bottoms down just far enough so she can point to the scar etched on her belly. It's a constant reminder of her days in what is now known as the Michener Centre in Red Deer, when she and many others were sterilized so they could not reproduce.

Carol Ann is officially classified as developmentally delayed. "I'm a slow learner," she says, with an impish gleam in her eyes. But in many ways, this 52-year-old woman is as smart as a tack.

A lifetime of trials has not dampened her spirit. Although she is bedridden and dying of cancer, she is playful, loving, generous, kind, and, yes, funny. The small circle of fiercely protective friends who surround her offer those adjectives to describe her, and those are the qualities that are immediately apparent when you meet her.

Carol Ann's former counsellor has become her friend and wants her story told—accurately and respectfully. Her lawyer says he is honoured to be in a position to act as her advocate. Her caregiver, who has taken Carol Ann into her home and made her a member of the family, says the story of this woman's life might inspire others.

Carol Ann has clearly won these three people over. Now she is keen to share details of her life with a wider audience.

She starts at the beginning—Milton, Nova Scotia, where she was born on July 10, 1953. Then right away she is recalling how she teased her younger brother. "I used to take his bottle away from him, to make him cry." The big brown eyes in her elfin face light up mischievously at the memory.

She's candid about her cancer. "It's in my kidneys…I'm not doing too good now…They can't do anything for me…I had a few treatments…They said no more…They're keeping me comfortable…My feet are numb now…I can walk, but not very good."

The cancer has spread to her stomach, liver and lungs. She underwent one operation and has endured chemotherapy treatments. But the doctors say their remedies are exhausted, so now a bag of morphine hangs beside her bed and she can push a button to turn the drip into a bit more when the pain becomes too intense. The machine in the corner of her basement room hums constantly as it pumps oxygen up the tubes to her nostrils. But, as she has all through her life, Carol Ann remains irrepressible. "I'm not going to die too easy," she vows, and the fact that she is still here in early 2006 is a testament to that. As her caregiver, Pearlin, puts it, "First we didn't think she'd make it through Christmas. Then we made it through Valentine's Day. Now we're aiming for Easter." Carol Ann is dreaming of a trip to SeaWorld in Florida, and Pearlin is not saying no. She talks about how she and Carol Ann used to play pool together, or watch movies, or "drive around laughing at licence plates." These two are clearly accustomed to overcoming obstacles and living through surprises.

This tiny woman with the huge brown eyes, the red polish on her fingernails and toenails, and the thin, gold-coloured bracelet is worth a small fortune. "I have lots of money," she offers. Details of the settlement she received from the Alberta government after a protracted dispute over her sterilization are subject to a confidentiality agreement, and it's a good bet that Carol Ann neither knows nor cares how much she's worth. She does, however, make a point of saying she has had her lawyer draw up her will. She says she never really wanted children anyway, but she's bitter that no one ever told her that she had been sterilized. "I was really mad about that. I lived my whole life without knowing. They didn't explain anything to me. You have to have it done or else you can't stay in here. Do you think I have a good story to tell?"

150

It's not easy for her to talk about what happened to her in Red Deer. Not because the memory is painful, but because details are blurred. At first she says she was there in 1955, but that doesn't add up, since she would have been two years old. She picks up the portable phone beside her bed and punches in her mother's number ("I talk to her three or four times a week"). "When was I in Red Deer?" "It was from 1965 to 1975," she is told —from the time she was 12 until she was 22.

"My mom couldn't take care of me at the time. My father drank. He used to come home drunk and hit my mom all the time. He hit me. He died of cancer."

Her memories of "Red Deer"—the Michener Centre, Alberta's Provincial Training School for Mental Defectives—are mixed. At first they're fairly positive, since she liked some aspects of the regimented lifestyle. "I wanted to stay in. I'd been protected all my life there. I was scared to come out. I liked the routine. But they figured it was best for me to come out."

But the more she talks, the more a dark picture emerges: "I didn't like being locked up. Six o'clock at night, you hardly had anything to do except watch TV and hang around."

And then: "They put me in a room with just four walls. One light. No shoes. A mattress on the floor. If you had to pee, you had to go right in your pants. In those days, they didn't care." Those "time out" rooms were infamous. "The punishment really gets to me. They put me in a jacket." She wraps her arms around herself to demonstrate. A straitjacket? "Yes, a straitjacket." So what had she done to warrant being put in the time-out room? "Maybe I broke a window." There were other women there, too, although the men were kept in a separate area. "They pulled my hair. You don't have your street clothes. You had to have bare feet. It was sometimes very cold on the floors."

"And then, they…" Words fail her. At this point, she reveals her scar, as though it could somehow tell the story for her.

It's impossible to say exactly what happened to Carol Ann in "Red Deer," but it's likely that the provincial Eugenics Board administered an IQ test and then ordered that she be sterilized. In all likelihood, her Fallopian tubes were cut, making it impossible for her to become pregnant.

"I'm really mad at them," Carol Ann says now. "I wish I knew more about myself. I'm delayed—mentally delayed. People have taken advantage of me." Even then, though, her streak of goodwill is evident. "I'm a slow learner, but it doesn't slow me down. I have a sense of humour sometimes, too. Isn't that right, Gail?" she asks her counsellor, who is sitting unobtrusively in the room for the first interview. The twinkle is there. Gail nods.

Alberta's Sexual Sterilization Act, passed in 1928, was based on the principles of eugenics, which is defined by the *Canadian Oxford Dictionary* as "the science of improving the (esp. human) population by controlled breeding for desirable inherited characteristics." The Alberta government and many activist groups and doctors at the time wanted to ensure that many "kinds" of people, including visible minorities and the "feeble-minded," were unable to reproduce.[1] In all, almost 3,000 Albertans were sterilized, including Carol Ann. The Act was not repealed until 1972.[2]

A lawsuit launched by Leilani Muir, who entered the Michener Centre as a youngster and was sterilized without her knowledge or consent, led to subsequent suits from hundreds of others. It's a matter of public record that Muir was awarded roughly $1 million in damages, interest and costs.

Carol Ann asks that the story of her life include a reference to the Centennial celebrations in a park in Red Deer in 1967. "Mom came down for it. Write about that." "Why?" "It's just a year that I remember very well. It was good for me." What's the best memory she has? "We went to Ontario and saw flowers in a park. I think that was my best moment."

Her second-best memory, she says, is of going to Gail for counselling. "She likes bugging me." Gail and Carol Ann chat about how someone was worried that Carol Ann was dangerously depressed and referred her. "When I met you," Gail remembers, "it was hard to get you to say nice things about yourself....Like the ad says 'you've come a long way, Baby.' You weren't always so kind to yourself."

Carol Ann nods in agreement. There's an obvious bond between them. Carol Ann says something about how she once took a life skills class. Then she asks if Gail might be able to find her poems, in case one or two might be worthy of inclusion in the book. (Gail does unearth the poems later. They are simple and focus mostly on love and loss and friendship.)

---

[1] http://www.canadiancontent.ca/issues/0299sterilization.html; james horner, sterilization and eugenics
[2] http://home.aol.com/lillithsrealm/myhomepage/Sterilization/ICSAIntr.htm

Other things light up Carol Ann's face as she talks. "I used to eat a lot of beans. Morning, noon and night. I didn't have any money coming in. Now I can eat what I want to eat." She flashes her delightful smile. "Chicken. Even Chinese food."

She takes great pleasure in her radio and television. "I like my music. Oldies. Rock and Roll Band. Sweet-sounding music. I tape songs off the radio…I'm good at taping the radio…You can get them on television too…I like game shows."

She reminisces about an old beau: "I used to have a boyfriend. But I dumped him. He used to pick up things out of garbage bags. I still talk to him once in a while. I'm a caring person. Once you know me, I would do anything for you."

She offers advice for young people: "Get a good education. In my time we didn't have any education in Red Deer. You can't get a job without it."

She also announces happily that she is "now a member of the Ottley club." Pearlin Ottley filled in as a daily living skills person for Carol Ann about six years ago. The two became friends and Pearlin ended up offering Carol Ann a room in the basement of her own home. As Pearlin puts it, "I had kids. I had an empty room. She moved in in 2001, and she never moved out."

The T-shirt Carol Ann so proudly wears is a souvenir from the trip the pair took to Barbados and Grenada in 2004. In early February, Pearlin was still packing Carol Ann into a wheelchair and pushing her through West Edmonton Mall. "I've always loved malls," Carol Ann pipes up enthusiastically.

Pearlin talks about how Carol Ann used to have real trouble controlling her anger, and Carol Ann agrees: "When I'd get upset, I'd put on headphones and yell and scream." She would also, in healthier days, walk for hours in the streets. "We worked through that." Pearlin says "Now she's going to tell you when she's mad." Pearlin sums up her friend this way: "She's awesome. She's kind. She has a big heart. For what she has been through, it's amazing she's doing so well."

Gail echoes this assessment of Carol Ann. She visits her frequently now, not as a counsellor, but as her friend. She was the one who urged that Carol Ann's story be included in this anthology, noting that telling a tale of hardship would not be uplifting, but adding that talking about her spirit, her courage and her willingness to survive is inspirational to those who know her. Carol Ann has endured great loss and often feels unlovable. But she is quick to smile, she appreciates help, she offers kind words and, as Gail puts it, she bears her sadness remarkably well. "She's a spunky, plucky gal."

Gail gets the last word:

"(Carol Ann) is not a saint, and in her younger days she certainly could get herself into difficult situations. But she has done her utmost to deal with life in a gracious way. She hasn't changed the world nor written a best-selling novel. Her legacy, for those who know her, will be that we will remember the lessons she taught about how to play the cards you are dealt in the best way that you can. If I can be anything like Carol Ann when it's my turn to go, I will have accomplished something."

by
Debby WALDMAN

No Holding Back

At lunchtime on a warm, sunny Friday in early spring, the Wye Gardens Dairy Queen in Sherwood Park is a hive of activity. The bright, clean dining room is filled with mothers and toddlers, seniors and grandchildren, students and workers, happily eating their midday meal. At the counter, a line of customers stretches almost to the door.

In the back of the kitchen, past the grill where workers assemble salads and sandwiches and fry up potatoes, chicken strips, and onion rings, Pamela West stands over a stainless steel sink, washing plastic food trays.

When she's finished drying them, she carries them out to the dining room, a rag and a bottle of antibacterial fluid in one hand. She deposits the clean trays, then sprays and wipes the newly vacated tables, cleaning them for the next customers. She checks the garbage cans to make sure they're not full. Then she picks up the dirty trays, carrying them back to the sink to start the routine anew.

Were it not for Pamela's efforts, the counter help wouldn't have trays to fill with food and the dining room would be an inhospitable mess. Yet she exudes a level of dutiful calm that makes you think she'd carry on in much the same efficient manner even if there were only a handful of customers.

Which is pretty much the case. "She's got a very good work ethic," says her boss, restaurant manager Brent Smith, who isn't joking when he refers to her as a workaholic. "She needs little, minimal supervision. She knows her job."

Even better, Pamela enjoys her job, which she started as part of a six-week work experience program at Bev Facey High School in 2001. Every afternoon, the grade eleven student learned to fold boxes, clean tables and package Dilly Bars. She was eager to learn and succeed, but the learning curve was steep. Ruth West, Pamela's mother, warned Smith that Pam would need to be repeatedly shown how to do her job.

"But once she learns her task, she never has to be told again," says Smith, who calls Pamela "the best of the bunch" of the work experience students he's had. "She knows exactly what she's doing. I don't know what her limitations are. I'm pretty darned sure she's not going to be able to run a cash register or take an order from customers, but she can fill pop for the orders and what not. She can bag and box novelties perfectly. I want her to start making them now. I'm going to keep going with her until she can't go any higher. Why hold her back?"

Pamela certainly doesn't have any interest in being held back. Her goal when she graduated from Bev Facey was to get a job. That's just what happened when Smith offered her full-time employment.

"Pamela will be here as long as she can stay," he says. "She's my best employee—no alcohol problems, no drug problems, no boyfriend problems, never late to work, doesn't lie, doesn't steal. You don't have to ask her three times. She just does it."

At twenty-three, Pamela enjoys the independence that comes with having regular employment. She walks the fifteen to twenty minutes to and from Dairy Queen five days a week, rain or shine, no matter what the temperature. She takes her paycheck to the bank and deposits it, and often spends some of her money on CDs and DVDs, adding to an already impressive collection.

The shelves in her bedroom downstairs at her parents' house are brimming with movies and music. Pictures of country music stars including an autographed picture and letter from local singer Adam Gregory are lined up next to glossy photos of figure skaters, among them Kristi Yamaguchi, Jamie Sale and David Pelletier, and Steven Cousins.

Pamela is a big figure skating fan. One of the highlights of her year is attending the "Stars on Ice" show at Rexall Place in the spring after eating dinner at her favorite restaurant, Swiss Chalet. Last spring Pamela began taking a skating-for-fun class. She also likes horseback riding and bowling.

To relax, she enjoys reading country music magazines and listening to CDs by George Strait, Terri Clarke, Shania Twain, Keith Urban, and Celine Dion. But it's clear from the size of her DVD collection that she is particularly passionate about movies. "I go crazy over this one," she says, holding up a box containing The Legend of Zorro before picking up The Mask of Zorro.

Pamela has enough DVDs and videos to open her own shop, and she loans many of her movies to her parents. But in a little over a year, Ruth and Bruce West will have to go further than their basement to borrow the flicks, because Pamela will be moving into her own home. She and her best friend Camille, a classmate since their grade seven special education class, are going to buy a Sherwood Park condominium.

It's a milestone the Wests couldn't have predicted when their daughter was diagnosed with developmental delays before her first birthday.

Pamela was the second of Bruce and Ruth's three daughters, born when their oldest, Cheryl, was three. Pamela's younger sister Laura, came three years after Pamela. As an infant, Pamela had a difficult time nursing and settling down. Ruth can't remember specifics, only that "she was obviously not developing as she should. I already had Cheryl and I knew the sorts of things to look for."

Doctors weren't able to pinpoint the cause of the delays, though an incident at the hospital shortly after Pamela was born, when she turned blue in her bassinet, may well have contributed. The doctors who diagnosed the delays provided little sense of what the Wests could expect from Pamela as she grew up. She began receiving therapy at the Glenrose Hospital. Because she wasn't speaking by the time she was two, she learned sign language, after which her spoken language developed quickly. However, she still doesn't pronounce all her words clearly. This can be especially frustrating because she isn't always understood and is often asked to repeat herself. She also continues to have challenges with her overall physical ability, manual dexterity, and fine motor skills.

Realizing Pamela would have limitations that their older daughter didn't, Ruth and Bruce reconsidered their expectations for her future. "I mourned the loss of what we had expected for Pamela, and in retrospect I would almost say I almost had to go through that to actually help her," Ruth recalls. "I accepted the fact that what was best for her was to be in a special ed' class and to be given that kind of education."

Looking back, Ruth believes it was "absolutely" the best choice she and her husband could have made for their daughter. "That was where she made her friends and certainly that's where she got the kind of instruction that she really needed—even the modified testing that she needed. She just needed to have some place where she could feel she was being successful."

Pamela went to Wye Elementary School in Sherwood Park, and then on to FR Haythorne Junior High and Bev Facey. In high school she was in a special education class with eleven other students for her core subjects, but she took a variety of options in a mainstream setting. Among her favorites were food preparation and horticulture. She wasn't so enthralled with hair care.

"It was a bit hard," she says of the class, where she was taught to use rollers, style hair, and do braids. When asked if there was anything in particular that she found difficult, she replies, without irony, "Mostly, everything."

She clearly took the challenges in her stride. Shy and soft-spoken, Pamela, who is small and pixie-like, with short brown hair and a sweet smile, stands straight and exudes a quiet confidence.

Asked to describe herself, she needs a bit of prompting before agreeing that she's organized, friendly, good to talk to, and polite. She's also highly dependable, a favourite worker at Dairy Queen, easy to get along with and pleasant to be around—unless, that is, she's getting unwanted attention.

One day about a year ago, some of Pamela's colleagues thought they'd help her out by giving her chores to keep her busy. However, they gave her so many she couldn't complete them. When she got frustrated, her co-workers tried comforting her—Smith says they were babying her— which frustrated her even more. Pamela got so fed up she marched into Smith's office and threatened to quit.

"I straightened people up right away," Smith recalls. "I said, I'm her boss. She's got one boss. And she's being pampered. She doesn't want to be babied."

Then he spoke with Ruth, who spoke with Pamela, who returned to work the next day. Smith assured her that she'd be treated as an equal, recognized for doing a good job, and given some space if she was in a lousy mood.

"At times like that, she just wants to be left alone," Ruth says. "She doesn't like the focus on her. We had this situation in school, too, and the teachers got to know very well—and Pamela got to know it, too—that the best thing for moments like that was to be by herself, to just have some time away, sit quietly for ten minutes or so, and then go back in."

Pamela's parents are confident that their daughter has developed and will continue to develop the skills she needs to look after herself and live independently. They're happy she's found a nice place to live, and a housemate with whom to share it, though neither expected her to leave home quite so soon. "We never tried to push her out—this was her choice," Bruce says. "The time was right."

Adds Ruth, "The fact is, even though she lives here she's quite independent. She takes care of her own laundry, buys her own food, makes her own breakfast. The only thing I'm doing for her is making her supper."

The condo complex, which is under construction, will be connected, underground, to a supportive living facility for seniors and those with physical disabilities. If Pamela and Camille choose, they can take some of their meals there.

Then again, the Wests point out, Pamela is a pretty good cook, and they're helping her expand her repertoire so she'll have a variety of dishes to choose from when she has her own kitchen. She can make Kraft dinner, pyrogies and cabbage, shrimp and pasta. Until her family decided to be more careful about cholesterol, she used to make brownies every week.

"She makes great brownies," her mother says, perhaps a bit wistfully.

She's also a good housekeeper, a skill she's honed making the rounds of the dining room at Dairy Queen. "It's nice to have her around the house," Ruth says. "She's very helpful."

"She does more cleaning than I do," jokes her father.

Pamela is looking forward to having her own apartment. She's planning to bring her bedroom furniture, TV, and the VCR/DVD player her parents bought her for Christmas. She and Camille, who works as a preschool aide, will likely have to buy a few more things to furnish the place, but given how much they have in common, it's doubtful they'll have trouble agreeing.

The two young women have known each other since junior high school and have been best friends for three years. They share a love and vast knowledge of country music, animals, and sports. Pamela has taken riding lessons and Camille's mother keeps horses at her acreage, along with a menagerie of dogs and cats. The two bowl together and take skating lessons. On Friday nights in the summer, you can often find them swimming at the Kinsmen Pool, or watching movies.

"At every stage in her life, Pamela has had a best friend," Ruth says. "She's had friends at school, kids who would come to birthday parties, and there certainly are those kinds of relationships now—at Dairy Queen there are people she enjoys working with—but her best friend now is Camille."

Settling into your first apartment can be traumatic. Leaving the comfort of your parents' home, the security of knowing that if something goes wrong there's a capable adult around to look after you—these are the sorts of doubts that often plague young adults on the eve of moving out. But Pamela, grounded and serious, has no qualms about her decision. Asked what she's looking forward to, she claps her hands, smiles broadly and says, "Camille and I are going to live together. I'll be happy."

Just as she's always been. And, given the support and love that surrounds her, will likely continue to be.

by
Curtis GILLESPIE

Just Trying to Make a Difference

Reporter's Notebook—facts/impressions: Greg Willson harbours a secret desire to be a writer. More specifically, he'd love to be a sports reporter, to have a notebook, to record what people say, what they do, how they perform, to record facts and impressions and then turn them into a story. You can tell as he talks about it that it would be a huge rush for him, kind of a fantasy. But you can also tell part of him is seriously working towards it, that he's not just playing at it.

Life is full of ironies; we all know that. Not a day goes by in this world that we don't take notice of one thing or another that makes us wryly shake our head at the incongruity of it all. One person who lives a kind of direct irony every day of his life is Greg Willson. Greg has cerebral palsy. This is just one fact about him. He is also a passionate and sympathetic person, a volunteer, a helper, a person who hears something on the news or sees it on TV, and doesn't just shake his head, but who says, "I've got to do something about that." And then he goes and does it. Greg sees things clearly, and he clearly sees a path of action before him. He is a man of vision. Greg Willson is also legally blind.

Music is central to his life. Country music is king, especially Faith Hill. Most nights he falls to sleep listening to her voice, to the words. He's also into the Dixie Chicks, and really pretty much any kind of country music. "It's in the blood," he says, laughing. He's heading to the Big Valley Jamboree at Camrose, in August, and it's already the highlight of his summer.

Reporter's Notebook—facts/impressions: Greg grew up in Spruce Grove, just outside Edmonton, and lived there for seventeen years, although his parents separated when he was ten, around the time his sister passed away. He has a twin brother. He gets along well with his family and sees and talks to them often. Clearly, he's like most of us—he wants to be both independent and connected, an individual and part of a larger unit.

Greg loves to write. It means a great deal to him, and it's something he really wants to get better at. To that end, he lets his reportorial instincts come to the fore through the Leduc Independent Living Services newsletter "LILS Today," in which he is both the editor and has a sports column entitled "Greg's Corner." Let's face it—the man is a sports fanatic. He loves the Oilers, and was cheering madly for them this past spring on their Stanley Cup run. Baseball is also right up there, and although he's not a regular he gets to games whenever he can down at Telus Field in the Edmonton river valley, back when the Trappers were in Edmonton and had a Triple A team and now with the Cracker Cats. "I love the field. I love going to a game, getting a corn dog, just enjoying the whole thing."

Greg was transported directly to the golden gates recently…well, if you're a baseball fan, that is. He went to Toronto for a family wedding and it was a fantastic trip all around which even included a trip up the CN Tower. Asked if he wasn't scared of the height, he lets his eyes widen. "No," he says. "I love heights!"

The highlight was being able to go to a Jays game with his aunt. "It was terrific," he says, smiling. "Would have been better if the Jays had won, but it was still great." He pauses, grins just slightly. "Would have been better, too, if the marriage had happened. Didn't quite work out. Great ball game, though." That little subversive sense of humour he's got slips through every now and then. You can see it when he says something you might take straight up for a few seconds, until that sly little smile breaks out from his lips, and when it does, you get that insight into what's going on up there.

The real cornerstone of who Greg is, and of how he defines himself, is through his work and his volunteering. He works part time at the Second Glance shop in Leduc. It's a used clothing shop, and he works doing tagging, moving and sorting material, basically anything that needs doing. He's been there for nearly three years, and he isn't going anywhere soon. He also works part time at the gift shop of the Leduc Community Hospital, where he handles customer service and runs the cash register, which was complicated at first, but now, he says, "It's a piece of cake!"

Greg is so into his work at the gift shop that he even bakes the cookies they sell there. "You bet," he says, smiling. "Macadamia, chocolate-chocolate chip, oatmeal raisin. It's not easy, either. They always want them just right."

Greg has always liked baking. "When someone's baking around the house, and I get to help out, I almost feel like it's a privilege. My mum used to bake and I would help her."

The other major factor in Greg's life—perhaps the biggest—is his volunteer work. But it's even more than that; it's about a state of mind, a way of being. Greg volunteers when and where he can. But he's an activist, too. That's his real calling. "It just feels really good to help other people," he says. "Like with the tsunami, or in Iraq. I just wish I could reach out more to them, to those people who are suffering. Sometimes, it's all so depressing it's even hard to start your day."

Greg has volunteered with the Great Human Race. He got sponsors for it. Greg is also really into the Low Rider bikes. He's made this a fundraiser, and actually organized a presentation to help raise funds to purchase a new Low Rider bike for himself. For those who are unfamiliar with the "low bike" it's a bicycle specially adapted for riders with some form of physical impairment, typically lower body mobility. Greg, for instance, has a lot of leg strength, but can't direct it towards riding a standard bicycle. Hence, the Low Riders.

His volunteering and social action impulse have also been stimulated with all the problems taking place in Iraq and Afghanistan, even in places like Pakistan and Indonesia for tsunami relief. "Just watching what some of the people go through when you see it, just on the news. It's terrible. You want to help." He stops for a minute, seems to think about it briefly. "How can you not want to help?"

Greg is also into the sense that we are all different, but all alike. The uniqueness we all have inside us is a gift we are meant to share with one another, but there are commonalities we can share, too. "I'm just so glad that we're all different," says Greg. "It would be so boring if we were all the same!"

Reporter's Notebook—facts/impressions: Greg's roommate, Danielle, is also one of his best friends. And he has a girlfriend, too, Shannon. "One of my dreams," he says, "is to live independently, in an apartment, with Shannon. That would be great." Note to self: Don't rule anything out when it comes to Greg Willson.

Greg is a busy guy, and an emotionally engaged person, too, which means that he feels things, takes them to heart—this all adds up to someone who can get worn down at times. Don't misunderstand, he has to have the motion and action. "I love it," he says emphatically. "I love being on the go. But I can't say that I don't get tired. Sometimes it feels like there are long days. That's when I like to just put my feet up, and relax."

It's no small irony, that Greg likes to help and that he also likes country music. After all, it was June Carter Cash, Johnny's wife, who, when people asked her how she was doing, would always reply, "I'm just trying to make a difference."

Greg loves his country music. And he loves just trying to make a difference. In a big way or a small way, it doesn't matter. What matters is the impulse. What matters is making a difference. And there's no doubting he's doing that.

by
Susan RUTTAN

An Obsession for Life

He sits on the living room floor, talking quietly to himself, occasionally singing softly in a pure high tenor. His eyes are fixed on the drawing paper on the coffee table in front of him. As he draws, his free hand is in constant motion, often fluttering in front of his eyes.

Drawing is James Doran's life. The sandy-haired twenty-four year old spends nearly every waking minute creating art.

On this day, a visit to his parents' home, James' drawing hand is stained with green ink from the coloured pen he's using to make his current creation. As soon as he fills a page, he starts again on another. He appears to ignore the conversation going on around him, unless prodded by his mother to respond to a question. He may be listening but he shows no interest in joining in.

Seen one way, James' drawing is the harmless obsession of a young man with autism, one that keeps him calm and manageable, perhaps even happy. Seen another way, James is an artist, plain and simple. His drawings have been sold—some for as much as $150. Twenty have been collected in a professional portfolio, complete with a description of each drawing—pencil crayon on paper, 2004; gel pen on paper, 2005; and so on.

Three days a week, James attends the Nina Haggerty Centre for the Arts, an Edmonton art studio for people with developmental disabilities. He was one of two artists from the Centre to have his work chosen by a panel of experts for display at the Abilities Festival in Toronto in

October 2005. James' drawing was one of eighty-one works from eight countries chosen for the four-day celebration of art created by people with disabilities.

Later, when James sold a drawing for the first time, his parents Margaret and Tim Doran were amazed. Then Margaret thought about the one that sold—gold and silver ink on black paper—and thought, "No, that was a nice picture." Several Doran family members now own pictures done by James, as does the SKILLS Society, the agency which manages his home, and Hazeldean Elementary School, where James was once a student.

The drawing that went to the Hazeldean school is a picture of New York City skyscrapers done in gold ink on black paper, with the words "New York" written above them. Most of James' pieces are more abstract than this. Many are drawings of an endless series of stacked boxes. Some have other shapes or words incorporated into them. Others have images drawn on top of earlier images, producing an eerie confusion of shapes.

"He doesn't recognize it as art," says his dad Tim. "I don't know that we recognize it as art. But some people do." Staff at the Nina Haggerty Centre, who are trained artists, have no doubt that James is creating art. "His art comes from somewhere that is a mystery to me," says Dave Janzen, artist-facilitator at the Centre, "but it's certainly got a petroglyphic thing about it." The shapes, Janzen says, are always architectural—skyscrapers, elevators, buildings, stairs.

James Doran has been drawing since he was a young child, an activity his mother introduced in order to distract him. Margaret remembers the first time she used drawing as a technique with her son. As a small boy he loved flushing the toilet obsessively for an hour or more continuously. "We just let him, so the water bill was high," Margaret Doran recalls. Obsessive behaviour is often part of autism, and this obsession seemed pretty harmless.

One day Margaret had to call the plumber to work on the toilet and James was shut out of his toilet-flushing for several hours. He began to have a tantrum. In order to calm him, Margaret drew a picture of a toilet in his sketchbook. The idea worked; the tantrum stopped. "He looked at the picture of the toilet, and thought, 'you can actually draw this,'" says Margaret. "He started to draw things from there on."

A few years later, James acquired a new obsession, for elevators. "He knew every elevator in every store and mall—and had to ride it," recalls his dad. Tim spent many a weekend taking his son from mall to mall to ride the elevators.

Then—as with the toilet obsession—the preoccupation with elevators morphed into drawing. It was here that James' interest in architectural shapes began to develop. Instrumental in the transition was a trip to New York that Tim Doran took in 1992. The pictures of Manhattan skyscrapers he brought back home fueled his son's imagination.

"James thought, 'all those buildings had to have elevators,'" says Margaret. "That's when this started."

'This,' is the art that James now creates. He draws elevators—and more elevators and more elevators. The stacked boxes in his drawings are elevators, as James himself will tell you if prodded.

Despite his success at the Abilities Festival and his ongoing work at the Nina Haggerty Centre, the road to becoming James Doran, artist, has been a difficult one.

James was diagnosed at 18 months as being developmentally disabled and started going to the Glenrose Rehabilitation Hospital for therapy. One day, his mother inquired about a job opening in the office of Glenrose autism specialist Dr. Catherine Lord. Lord gave Margaret a book on autism in preparation for the job interview. As she read it, Margaret realized she was reading about her four-year-old son. She went back to Lord and asked for help. After an extensive evaluation, Lord confirmed that James was autistic.

Autism is a neurological disorder that affects the areas of social interaction and communication skills. At its most severe, according to the Autism Society of Canada, people with autism have symptoms of extremely repetitive and unusual behaviours that may include self-injury and aggression.

James' condition made him a difficult youngster. He threw tantrums, banged his head on the floor, punched holes in the walls of the family home, and was aggressive with his younger brother Connor.

The Dorans were determined to help James become the most he could be. Margaret started teaching him sign language, starting one day with the sign for "cookie."

"The next day I was looking at him in the kitchen, and he was over there practicing with his hand. He was trying to say the word cookie."

Margaret knew then that her son could learn to communicate. She started teaching him other sign words, and later, to talk.

When he was old enough to attend school, James became one of the first autistic children in Edmonton to be integrated into a regular classroom, accompanied by a full-time aide.

"I was really concerned," recalls Margaret, "because he had a lot of extreme behaviours at the time, but the teacher was very, very interested in doing this, which was the key." James remained integrated throughout elementary school, then spent his teenage years in special programs. By that time, he was living in the group home that the Dorans had helped establish. Caring for a child as challenging as James had become too hard for the family.

"It did become physically very difficult for me to keep him under control," says Margaret.

James was eight years old when he went to live in the home. The decision to place him there had been heart-wrenching. Yet the Dorans knew that as their son got older and physically stronger, his physical outbursts would pose a danger to both his brother and his petite mother.

"You sit down and try to make the right decision, then you second-guess yourself for five years," Margaret says. "It's hard."

The Dorans found a house in central Edmonton, got government funding and found a roommate—a child James' age who also attended the Hazeldean preschool. Later, a third child joined them and together they moved to a house in south Edmonton, just a five-minute drive from the Dorans' house.

"It's allowed us to stay very close to James, which is what we wanted," says Margaret. "We in no way wanted to hand him over to someone and say, 'raise him'."

Today James can talk, although he rarely chooses to do so. He can write and read. His staff write his month's activities on a calendar which he reads religiously, insistent that everything on it happen exactly as planned.

He can sing "O' Canada" in French and can remember the names of his first therapist and first psychiatrist. He can tell you the plot of his favourite movie, *Mr. Holland's Opus*, and make up stories about imaginary people. However, James is classified as a total dependent, because he can't take care of himself. He will sometimes go into the bathroom and forget why he's there, says Diane Hannah, team leader for James' home. A staff member will have to go in and tell him to take his clothes off and have his bath.

The home is staffed round the clock and James has a fulltime aide, Neil Amyotte, who takes him to the Nina Haggerty Centre, supplies him with paper and pens for his art, and keeps him calm and safe. James also visits his parents every Wednesday and every third weekend. He doesn't stay the night. At twenty-four, he is an adult and has his own home.

The three young adults in the house share their home with Mini, a plump tabby cat. Diane Hannah says James and Mini get along fine. When Mini jumps up on his drawing paper he shoos her away, but doesn't become agitated. "She seems to follow him around a lot when he's upset," says Hannah. "If he's down in his room and he's upset, rest assured she's down there with him."

James' personal challenges did not end with the move to the supported living situation. "When I started working with James he was off the wall," says Diane Hannah. "Mind you, I guess puberty had a lot to do with it."

Tim can remember weekends when James would come home for a visit and walk from room to room for four hours straight. Tim would have to follow him to make sure James didn't lose control and become destructive.

In one particularly bleak episode, James was sent to the psychiatric unit at the Royal Alexandra Hospital. He needed six people to hold him down. "He was so out of control that they had to post a security guard outside his door," recalls Tim. "It was very distressing for all of us."

About seven years ago, the difficult behaviours began to be replaced, gradually at first, by drawing. Diane Hannah thinks one reason was the changed view that those around him began having of James' drawing. "We always felt his drawing was an obsessive thing, and we tried to draw him away from it and get him involved in things that were happening around him," she says. "Now that we understand that this is his passion, we respect that." That respect arose out of the work of an art student at James' home. The student taught the other staff to view James' work as art, not as obsessive scribbling. Today James is free to draw for eight or ten hours a day. His staff and parents make sure there's a limitless supply of paper and coloured pens, so he'll never run short.

James' style has evolved over the years, according to Diane Hannah. When James was younger he would simply fill his pages with written words. Staff could tell when James was building up for an emotional explosion by his drawings. "He would write in really dark pen, and fill the whole page up so it was dark, dark writing," says Hannah.

Now words are an occasional element, not the dominant feature of James' work. The evolution in his style may be due, in part, to his involvement with the Nina Haggerty Centre. The Centre is a busy place full of several dozen people sitting at tables painting, drawing and making pottery. James is clearly at home there. He doesn't interact with others, but he's comfortable as he sits working on his drawing, with his aide Neil at his side.

It was at the Centre that James really started being treated as an artist. "He's fully accepted in that place," says his mother.

James has little interest in his art once it's done, say those around him. It's the act of drawing, not the end result that matters. Even the money he's earned has no reality for him, although Diane Hannah did treat him to a spending spree at an art store with the proceeds from one sale.

Recently, she has noticed that James is starting to bring his drawing home. "You begin to wonder if he sees more in them," Hannah says. As others put more value on James' drawings, perhaps he's beginning to as well.

The Dorans look at their son the artist today and marvel. Margaret remembers James' psychiatrist telling her, when he was a troubled nineteen-year-old, that by twenty-five her son would be completely settled down. She didn't believe it then. Now she sees James quietly pouring himself into his drawings, hour after hour, and she's become a believer. "Where he is right now is better than we'd ever hoped he'd be."

by
Heather MARSHALL

Mister In-Between

"Do you want to see the fort I'm building?" asks Matthew Ambeault. The twenty-three-year-old is taking a break from his chores and wants to show me what he's been working on. We walk along the fence and come to a path. We scramble through a few metres of underbrush. Following the line where wild grasses and poplar saplings meet wheat stubble, he takes me to his refuge.

"There are no nails in this fort," he says. "When the farmer wants to push it into the bush, he won't have nails being a problem. I've tied all the sticks together with twine."

He indicates the grass he's using for the roof, the sticks that form the structure, and the log inside that he likes to sit on. "I like to have a place to sit when I have a smoke," Matthew informs me. He crawls inside, sits on his log, and lights up a cigarette. "I like coming here, just to get a break and to have smoke." We sit in silence on the line between two habitats. As Matthew gazes out across the expanse of farmland I wonder where the view takes him.

Matthew works for Suzanne Bryson at Stone Country Farms, her Welsh pony stable near Leduc. Suzie has taken Matthew on as a stable hand, but she also wants to prepare him to get a job working with horses at other equine facilities. Matthew has some challenges with learning and staying focused, but you would never guess it to look at him. A handsome, poised young man, he would fit in with any crowd of young people hanging out at Starbucks. His challenges only become apparent as you get to know Matthew—as he reveals his in-between life, caught between the things he can do and the things he can't.

We first meet on a brisk November morning at Stone Country Farms. Matthew is busily loading hay onto a dolly. Suzie introduces us, then leaves to do her own share of the work. Matthew pushes the dolly down to the stable yard, where all sizes and shapes of Welsh ponies are kept. He opens a gate into a corral that contains about twenty horses, each determined to get food first. He talks and whistles and cajoles the ponies to behave themselves as they tussel to be the ones to get the first sheaf of hay. He confidently moves among them, talking softly, sometimes reprimanding this one or that for biting another pony. Speaking to each one by name and liberally handing out treats, he takes time to visit with his favorites. He throws out more hay, then moves on to the next corral.

Matthew works at the farm four days a week, eight hours a day. It's his job. "I'd rather be here seven days a week if I could," he says. "I really like it here, being with the horses." He hopes to get a job as a barn manager someday.

Suzie provides Matthew with a list of the chores he is expected to do: clean out stalls, haul hay to corrals and feed horses, fill water tanks, assist with training younger horses, greet visitors and catch horses for young riders' lessons. The list is long and Matthew holds his own in carrying out all the things that are asked of him.

Midway through feeding, Matthew realizes that his blood sugar is low. We go into the meeting and coffee room, where he tests his blood sugar levels, then consumes an over-sized peanut butter and banana sandwich. "I've been eating these since I was five," he reveals. "The funny thing is, I hate bananas. I think they are gross by themselves. But these sandwiches are the best."

Suzie comes in, wondering what Matthew is up to. She tells him that he needs to get back to work and that if he is going to take a break he needs to let her know when and why. His reaction is like that of a teenager—some eye-rolling, defensiveness, and a "Yes mom" type of retort. Yet he listens to what Suzie has to say and moves quickly onto his next batch of chores, finishing up the feedings and filling up the water tanks.

Suzie is working nearby, cleaning stalls. She talks about the importance of keeping Matthew to his schedule. "He needs to have a regular routine, and I try to make sure he gets it here," she says. "If something happens to break the routine, we're often right back to square one." Suzie ensures that Matthew does his chores in the same order every day and that his breaks come at the same time each day. She also has an incentive program for Matthew—lunch in town on Thursdays. Her brother owns a sports car and Matthew loves it. So every Thursday, providing that the week has gone well and Matthew has done his work properly, Suzie and her brother take Matthew to town in the sports car. "This gives Matthew a chance to talk about cars, which he really enjoys," she says. "It works pretty well as a way to keep him on track during the week."

While the water tanks are filling, Matthew sweeps out the stable and talks about himself. He lives in Edmonton with his parents. Does he have brothers or sisters? "I wish!" he says. However, he does have a worker named Dave that he hangs out with. Sometimes they go to the swimming pool, lift weights, or play basketball. Occasionally, they make a fire at the park, roast some wieners and do a little fishing. At one time they did some body work on a car, using parts Matthew had found for Dave on the Internet.

Matthew is gifted with computers. "I've only ever taken one computer course, but for some reason I am really good at using them," he says. Matthew spends much of his free time on the Internet. "The thing I don't get," he says, "is how come I can do so much with computers—I can even do programming—but they say my IQ is low. Why is that?" Nevertheless, he can spend hours playing games like chess or pool with other people on the computer.

According to his mom, Matthew's school career was not an easy one. His intellectual disability was not easily diagnosed and he was often labeled as lazy. He has good long term memory and is highly verbal. However he has difficulty focusing and his low intellectual ability prevents him from doing many of the tasks expected in a school setting. When Matthew was finally diagnosed with Pervasive Developmental Disorder, his difficulties became more understandable and his parents were able to get him into programs that enabled him to progress.

While attending a private school on a farm in Ontario when he was eight, Matthew got first hand experience of rural life. Part of the program involved looking after the chickens, cats, dogs and a horse. To help him focus on learning to read, he was only allowed to go to the barn after his phonics exercises were complete. This incentive not only helped him to learn to read, but it also encouraged the love for animals that is so evident today in his relationship with horses.

During his teens, Matthew and his family lived in Montreal. According to his mother, Matthew learned to speak French "just like a Frenchman" although he was unable to learn to read the language. While in a music therapy program, Matthew showed improvement in his ability to listen and to focus his attention. He took guitar lessons, learning about eighty songs that he would practice and play over and over again. Music was a big part of his life as a teenager.

Matthew was in a life skills program, but was bored with it, so quit school sometime in grade eight or nine. The rest is all a blank to him, says Matthew. "Maybe it's the medications, the challenges, or other stuff." Around this time he began horseback riding. When he was nineteen, Matthew's parents bought him a horse of his own. He and his horse competed in local equestrian events. They took a number of ribbons, including one first place.

Every Friday night, Matthew and his Dad go to a movie—it's their "guy time" together. Matthew usually picks the movie and is quite clear that he doesn't want to see any PG stuff. He prefers things with lots of action and blood. "I don't know why I like that kind of show. Maybe it's because a babysitter showed me *Pet Cemetery* when I was five. I remember a scene from that movie, and that's what I like."

The floor swept, Matthew is ready for a coffee break. He goes into the coffee room, pours out a large mug of coffee, then offers to show me his fort. As we stand at the fence line looking out over the field, I ask him what it is he likes best about working with the horses. "I can't really say," he says. "It's just a feeling. I just feel so different when I am near them. They make me feel different." "Is that a good feeling?" "Yes, it is. A very good feeling."

The fence that separates field and bush stands between two landscapes. Matthew is also between places. On one side he is fully able to function with the responsibilities of his job, and yet not able enough to go it alone. The line between ability and inability, between maturing boy and young man is blurred, and his gaze is one of bewilderment at this in-between place.

Matthew and I meet for second time, a few weeks later. He has left his work with Suzanne Bryson and taken another job. His new boss is Karen Able, owner of Dawnville Farms, another stable located nearer Leduc. It is in a more convenient location for his mother, who drives him from Edmonton to his work site five days each week. But there are other reasons for the shift. "I just needed a change," says Matthew. "I felt like I was being given too much responsibility, and I wanted to be treated like an adult. It felt sort of like school."

His new work sits well with him. It comes easily and he is good-natured about doing it. Not only that, he likes the slightly higher pay and the fact that he gets to spend most afternoons riding the horses once all of the morning chores are done. Matthew has also been given the opportunity to use a pellet gun to shoot pigeons. "I haven't hit one yet," he says. "I will eventually."

Like Suzanne Bryson, Matthew's new employer provides him with a list of tasks to be done daily, and she ensures that he performs up to her expectations. He feeds and waters the horses, cleans stables, sweeps floors and moves the horses from stall to corral and back again. The desire to ride the horses in the afternoon provides all the incentive he needs to do a good job.

No longer working with small ponies, the horses at Dawnville Farms tower over Matthew. I ask him how he likes working with the larger animals. "I love them just the same," he says. It's clear that Matthew has already developed relationships with these animals and he is fearless. Calling them by name, feeding them treats, and catching them in the outdoor corral comes so naturally to him that it's hard to believe he's only been here a short time.

There are other changes afoot. Next month Matthew will be moving to a supported home in Leduc. With the move, Matthew will begin a new chapter of independence from his family, and open up opportunities for new things to learn. Perhaps the "good feeling" that he gets around the horses will keep him focused. As he moves toward his goal of greater independence and a possible career in the horse industry, having one foot in a place of ability and the other in that place of inability may no longer be so bewildering.

by
Allan CHAMBERS

The Perfect Blue

Leona Clawson is seeking a perfect blue, the lighter-than-sky colour of angel wings, but at the moment it exists only in her imagination. Her dark brows furrowed, eyes intent, she dips her brush into a well of white paint and brings it to a palette where a patch of paint is waiting to be transformed. "I want a real light blue," she says slowly, studying the effect as the white paint spirals into the blue and a more complex hue begins to emerge.

She wears denim jeans and a denim apron, which lends a certain jauntiness to her large frame. Bent over a sculpture or a painting, she is all business. Thick oval glasses accent her serious features. When she finds the right colour, a smile transforms her face and makes her look much younger than her fifty-eight years.

Around Leona, other artists are engaged in similar missions, mixing colours, assessing their impact, heads nodding to the Elton John tape as brushes flutter among the colours and glazes: holly green, Aztec brown, chartreuse, navy, burgundy, fire engine red, blue fire. There is conversation among the ten or so artists but it is low and gentle, comforting. The air is intense with concentration, yet it is tranquil. The feeling is of an artisans' studio from another time; the engagement between artists and their work is total.

We are in the clay studio at the Nina Haggerty Centre for the Arts, located on a busy avenue at the northern edge of Edmonton's inner city. I have the good fortune to be balancing on a wobbly stool at a cluttered table between Leona and her close friend Lisa. Leona is painting an angel she has sculpted. Lisa, a quiet woman born in Hong Kong, is working on a bowl.

Leona has been coming to the Centre since it opened in 2003 as a creative space for artists with disabilities. Like Nina Haggerty, the Centre's namesake, Leona spent much of her life in an institution before discovering in art a purpose and a doorway to self-expression. She is a prolific artist. The Centre is both her workplace and a second home—as much of a home, perhaps, as her tiny room in a group home in north Edmonton, where her "studio" once consisted of a card table.

The perfect blue that Leona seeks is beginning to show hints of itself. "Should there be more white?" she asks. "I want to put more white in there." She addresses the question to herself, to Lisa, to the air around us. It's Lisa who responds. "I like that idea," she says in her low, rapid voice. "I like the way she picks her colours. I think it's amazing. Right, dude? I always call you dude. 'Go wash your hands, dude. They're all white'."

They talk like this throughout the morning, two friends absorbed in their art. Elton John is replaced by the Backstreet Boys who are replaced by Britney Spears. Lisa confides that she dreams of returning to China. Leona considers this. "I'd like to go places," she says. "I'd like to travel, but I can't do that and paint too." She rinses her brush in a yogurt container filled with water, returns to the well of white paint. "Painting is a kind of travel, I guess. You can travel when you paint because you can go away in your mind, think of what colours you're going to find. So it's like traveling."

Leona speaks meditatively, each word measured. In the sixth grade, she was judged to be a slow learner. She suffered from frequent epileptic seizures. Leona was sent from Edmonton to the Michener Training School in Red Deer. At 13, she was sterilized without her permission. Her parents, who signed the papers, were told the operation would quiet the seizures. It didn't. The experience left her with an indelible sense of injustice. Today she is an advocate for the rights of the powerless, the second-class, the unnoticed. Her words are spoken slowly, but carry the force of direct experience, of her own memories of helplessness, of life decisions made without her approval.

"Once you went into that place (Michener), you didn't have any rights," she says. "For instance, the right to say no. When I was at Michener, they weren't supposed to do that operation. But they still did it under the table. They didn't ask me. They just did the operation." She regrets the lost opportunity to have children. "It is a very big regret. I didn't want that operation."

There is a silence. Leona's expressive face reflects her sadness. The strong jawline, though, suggests a combative spirit. That is perhaps what rescued her in the end, turned her into an artist and an implacable advocate for human rights. But now she smiles. "I think I've got my colour," she says, examining the transformed blue on her palette. "I don't very often get my colour like that."

Lisa watches carefully as the light blue is brushed onto the angel's wings. "My grandmother died and it was very hard on us," she says. "Now I think she's an angel. But I don't know much about angels. What are angels for?"

Leona considers this. "I don't know either," she says.

They are both silent as Leona paints the angel's wings. "Angels should stick together," she finally says.

In 2003, Leona Clawson was part of a project that linked the arts with issues of human rights involving persons with disabilities. Nina Haggerty artists, guided by professional artists Paul Freeman and Harold Pearse, examined human rights and citizenship issues in the light of their own experience. Besides individual works of art, they jointly created a model city to illustrate the obstacles that undermine the pursuit of human rights. The project led to a trip to Ottawa by the artists to meet John Ralston Saul, spouse of then Governor-General Adrienne Clarkson. A documentary film, *Through the Eyes of Artists*, captured the aspirations of the artists and the moving response of Saul, a writer with an interest in human rights.

In the spring of 2005, Ralston Saul repaid the visit by coming to the Nina Haggerty centre and by writing a forward to a book about the centre's artists and its human rights project. "Everyone—including people with disabilities—has something to contribute to society," he wrote. The work of the Nina Haggerty artists, he said, "will help us see the world through their eyes, if only for a moment, and hopefully discover a different consciousness."

Leona was a natural for the project. Her art is on frequent display at the Centre. Her acrylic paintings are unmistakable, their colours vibrant, the themes of country scenes and rambling homes immediately recognizable. Some operate at a deeper level. A painting entitled *Free as a Bird* depicts birds flying over water, watched by a human figure on a beach. The soaring wings of the birds speak of a freedom that the figure on the beach can only imagine.

During the eight months the Centre's artists worked to define rights issues for themselves, and to set out their own conception of community and human responsibility, Leona was often dubious about what they would achieve. How could art affect community perceptions? Would anybody even notice the efforts of people with disabilities whose very lives are a struggle for recognition of any kind? Among the participating artists, she became known as the questioner, the doubter.

The trip to Ottawa was an adventure. Leona loved it. Her group visited Rideau Hall, had tea with Ralston Saul under a summer tent on the beautiful grounds, discussed art and rights. "I had a lump in my mouth," Leona confesses. "It was exciting, but then again I was nervous."

She was not nervous enough, however, to surrender her own judgment. Although the rights project is completed, "I haven't seen anything new," Leona says. "I'd like to see us get more recognition, in other words, noticed more in what we do."

Lisa interjects. "I think you are changing that," she says.

Leona considers this, dips her brush in the yogurt container, speaks slowly. "Through my art I'm getting noticed," she says. "What I mean is disadvantaged people. Everybody should get noticed a little bit more. People should become more aware of other people, and accepting too. We'll see what happens. Maybe that will happen."

When Leona was a young woman, her mother—also an artist—gave her some painting supplies and suggested she try them. The gift changed her life. She gained more than the brushes and paints her mother had used before her. She gained a voice. "I'm very grateful to her," Leona says. "She still paints, but not much. I'm the one that keeps the painting going. I'll be painting probably for the rest of my life. Every time I pick up a brush, I always remember her."

Leona's parents, both elderly, live on Edmonton's south side and are in frequent contact with their daughter. Leona also has a sister and a brother in Edmonton. She had a twin sister, Lynn, who died recently. Leona misses her twin sister, but a connection remains. "I feel closer to her now than I did when she was alive," she says, with wonder in her voice.

Leona's mother found the Nina Haggerty Centre for her. Leona remembers the first time she stepped into the Centre, after having tried with frustration to paint in the small room in her home.

"My breath was taken away," she said, recalling that first visit to the Centre. "I thought, 'Oh my.'"

On another winter day at the Centre, Leona roams between the main painting room and the clay studio. "I have a lot of paintings here," she says, removing a sheaf of unframed paintings from a shelf, shuffling through the brightly-coloured works. "A lot." At the Centre, she moves with ease and some authority. She has earned it. This is her workshop, her element. Her paintings hang in the Stollery Gallery, the main display space. Her riveting clay mask is on the wall. A set of clay tiles depicting a story of encounters with a bear, is also on display. It recently sold for $130. "I'm in the money," Leona said, chuckling, when the cheque was handed to her by Wendy Hollo, the Centre's director.

Back in the clay studio, Leona picks up a bowl that she is working on. The search for the right colour begins again. She settles into her work, with its gentle rhythms, and talks reflectively about her art and her life. She left the Michener Centre after ten years, when she was twenty-three. For about a year she moved among several institutional homes before settling into an Edmonton continuing care institution for thirteen years. From there, she moved to the supported home where she now lives.

"I used to be a person who was very nervous," she says. "I wouldn't do a lot of things. But now, changes have come and I'm doing a lot of things, letting things happen. I was scared to let anything happen."

At the centre, the artists talk on tape and sometimes on camera about their work. Uneasy at first, Leona is now comfortable discussing her art, colours, life. "I'm still scared that nobody's going to recognize me and understand me. That's the biggest thing—understanding."

Leona has a deeply-rooted fear, stemming from her childhood years at the Michener Centre. She cautiously approached that fear in a painting, titled *My Life*, that depicts two figures on a floor contending together with an epileptic seizure. Each of the figures is a part of herself. "I'm still scared of that picture," she says. "I'm scared to go back there. I don't want to go back."

She returns her attention to the scene she is creating on a clay bowl. "The sun is going to shine," she decides aloud. "There has to be a darker blue."

Leona doesn't know where her colours come from. They appear first in her imagination, leading her on a search with her brush to try to capture them. In the process, she has learned patience. She has learned to relax. "People who are so busy working, they should paint," she says. "It gets the anxiety out. That's why I think everyone should paint."

In the clay studio at the Nina Haggerty Centre, anxiety seems—on this day at least—to be a concept from another world. There is a quiet creativity in the air. The artists breathe it, share it. One wants the chartreuse glaze. Another surveys a bowl from different angles, holding it high. Leona Clawson bends over her own work and imagines the right shade of blue. Time doesn't seem so important. There are lessons here that the rest of the world could learn.

by
Mark HAROUN

Springtime for Brent

The rain hasn't let up all week. I'm beginning to believe the sun will never make its appearance. But the rain has its positive side; in drought-ridden Alberta, everything is suddenly turning green again. The lush green is particularly evident in St. Albert, where towering birch trees and manicured lawns seem to line every street. I drive down Boudreau Road, rain streaking my windshield, looking for the home of Brent Hickey, the 58-year-old man who I'm planning to interview today.

Brent's neighborhood is fairly typical of St. Albert. There are well-cared for bungalows and two-storey homes with two-car garages, basketball hoops, and the odd tricycle lying abandoned in a driveway. I wonder if the neighbors are aware that a different sort of family lives in the large house at the end of the street—a home where *mother, father, sister* and *brother* take on different meanings. That home is run by the Lo-Se-Ca Foundation. It has been divided into several smaller homes designed to support the independence of people with developmental disabilities. One of these "homes within a home" belongs to Brent Hickey. He has lived there for eight months. Previously, Brent lived in a group home with three other men and received twenty-four-hour support from care workers. While he still receives some support (about twenty hours per week), Brent is more independent than ever before. He is now an official bachelor, complete with his own bachelor pad.

I park in front of the house and then slosh my way to what I assume is the door to Brent's basement apartment. I knock several times, but there is no answer. It's starting to rain harder now, and just as I'm about to run back to my car, Sherry Monczunki—the home's support team leader—arrives to greet me. She takes me to the correct entrance, a large glass door opening onto a set of concrete stairs leading downward.

When I meet Brent, I am surprised at how young he looks. At fifty-eight, he is around the same age as my parents who I regard as being, well, old. But despite thinning hair and a few well-earned wrinkles, Brent's exuberance belies his age. He credits his attitude to life for giving him a youthful appearance, describing himself as a "happy go lucky" guy.

With such youthful energy and those sparkling blue eyes, I'm not surprised when Brent announces that he has a girlfriend. Mind you, he hasn't met her yet, at least not in person. They've been communicating over the phone for several weeks (Brent assures me that her mother approves). He explains, "She's mad about me, she kept me on the phone for thirteen hours." I was previously warned by Sherry that Brent has a tendency to exaggerate, but in my experience when it comes to big emotions like love, over-exaggeration is a prerequisite. One should love big, and thirteen hours on the phone is only a basic penance to Cupid's arrow. Hopefully, it wasn't a long distance call.

All in all, Brent's basement suite is a pretty decent bachelor pad. His kitchen is especially well-equipped, with chrome appliances and various utensils. There's a comfortable sitting room and a healthy-sized television set for watching hockey. I've lived in my fair share of basement apartments, and they've all had two things in common: an absence of natural light and a chill dampness that no amount of heaters or dehumidifiers could mask. But Brent's apartment isn't like that at all. There is a positive vibe in the room, no doubt a result of Brent's bigger-than-life personality and even bigger laugh. You can't help but be buoyed up by such positive energy. The spring in his step is especially profound today, and can only be attributed to the mysterious woman on the other end of the phone. Brent is already making plans to meet her in person at his home. Sherry interjects that inviting a girl home on the first date may not be the best idea. She explains, "I have a boyfriend, and if he had invited me to his home on the first date, I would not have been very impressed." Wise advice, I think. I myself have always subscribed to the three-date rule: nobody goes home with anyone until at least the third date. I suggest taking her to a movie instead. Brent however, doesn't seem particularly interested in my advice. It's probably for the best, considering that my own dating track record is less than spectacular.

Sherry leaves us alone to chat. I turn my attention to the drum set. "Do you play?" I ask. A silly question considering that there are two drum sets in the room, one at the end of the stairs and the other near the kitchen. "Since I was eighteen," Brent replies with a smile, "I saved up all the money so I could buy it on my own." The older drum set near the stairs is rarely used, but the other is Brent's prize possession. He shows me a picture of himself playing in a rock and roll band. "I'm really good," he assures me. I ask Brent if he'll play for me, but he's not too keen on the idea. "I'd have to warm up first."

Music plays a central role in Brent's life. His well-stocked collection of old records contains the likes of BB King, The Rolling Stones, Elvis, The Guess Who, Queen and Michael Jackson. And what collection would be complete without The Beatles? "I can't believe people used to burn their records," Brent laments, referring to the conservative backlash that resulted when John Lennon was quoted as saying his band was more popular than Jesus. In Brent's words, their music "shows me history." As far as musical role models go, he has a hard time deciding which is his favourite. He eventually settles on Michael Jackson's *Thriller* because, "It makes me want to move."

When Brent isn't playing music, he's a fiercely competitive bowler. Just ask Samuel Mawutor, Brent's support worker. "He almost always wins. He has a very competitive spirit." Samuel is slowly learning the more technical aspects of the game from Brent. "When I do win, I have to celebrate so I do a little dance," he explains. Brent doesn't like it when Samuel wins, but the dance sends him into hysterics every time. To balance out the wins and losses, they've added Chinese checkers into their weekly routine. So far, Samuel is the reigning checkers champion, but Brent is learning quickly and it won't be long before he is doing his own victory dance. When Brent talks about Samuel, he refers to him as a friend, which speaks volumes about the open and caring relationship between the two men. According to Samuel, "Brent is always himself, he doesn't hide anything."

Brent is grateful to those who have helped him on his journey towards independence. If Samuel is the big brother, then Sherry is the mother hen. Brent describes her as: "Calm, cool and collected," and then adds, "she should get a raise." Brent's appreciation of those who support his lifestyle motivates him to help the less fortunate. Sherry often observes Brent reaching out to the elderly, or those who have greater physical or mental challenges. He is a source of reassurance and friendship for a deaf man who lives in the home. Although Brent isn't able to sign, his smiles and pats on the back go a long way. Brent's own struggle with diabetes has instilled in him a profound social conscience. "My heart goes out to people who have diseases. I want to help." Not surprisingly, one of his heroes is Terry Fox. Like Brent, Terry Fox had a disability but didn't let it stand in the way of going after his dreams.

Despite Brent's seemingly endless positive energy, he is somber as he shows me a wrinkled photograph. "This is Sunny, he was my best friend." After a moment Brent continues, "He was suffering from a lot of pain. It's hard for me to talk about him without crying." Sunny died earlier this year. His death is not the only loss that Brent has endured. Both his mother and father have passed away. Especially painful was the loss of his mother, with whom Brent shared a close bond. But when it comes to his own mortality, Brent is quick to say, "I'm not ready. There's a lot of stuff left that I want to do."

It doesn't take long for the tone of the conversation to revert back to its former giddy excitement. Brent turns his attention to the mysterious woman he seems to be very much in love with: "My mom told me I should get married to a nice girl. I might get down on my knees (and say) 'Look, I love you with all my heart.'" Brent's words are so genuine and heartfelt that I can't help but let go of my own cynicism. Perhaps this girl will eventually become everything Brent hopes she will be: a partner, a wife, and somebody who will always be there, no matter what. Brent makes everything seem possible.

"I'm going uphill," Brent tells me. At first, I'm not sure what he means. But as the conversation progresses, I begin to understand. Brent desperately wants what most people take for granted: a job, independence, friends, and a devoted life-partner. His disability makes obtaining all of these things an uphill battle, but not an impossible one. At times, obstacles have been placed in his way. He doesn't want to go into details, but Brent tells me that he has been taken advantage of—personally and financially— by those who prey upon people with disabilities. He has had to learn the hard way that not everybody has good intentions. Yet, like a true mountaineer, Brent is willing to suffer the scrapes and bruises incurred by the steep climb towards independence. "I am a guy that does not give up," he says, and because of this determination, his dreams are beginning to come true. Brent now has his own apartment, trusted friends, many social engagements and now, the possibility of love. It is truly springtime for Brent.

By the time I drive away from his home and head back towards Edmonton, the rain has finally let up and the sun is starting to peek through the clouds. As the lush lawns of St. Albert fade into the cement and asphalt of the highway, I recall the framed words hanging on Brent's wall, "Fiery, steep hill. Solid as a rock: wants to succeed without the help of anyone and will stop at nothing to fulfill his dreams."

The following week, I return to St. Albert to visit Brent again. This time, his mood is not quite so cheerful. Things didn't work out with the girl on the other end of the phone line. Brent's heart is broken. He has not been able to sleep at night. I tell him that broken hearts take time to heal, but such words are cold comfort when love is lost. I change the subject and again try to persuade him to play the drums for me. Brent says no at first, but then changes his mind. He sits down and begins to play, eyes closed, head back, mouth open. Just for a moment, he forgets his broken heart and his daily uphill battle, and allows himself to be transported back to his happy-go-lucky self, one beat at a time.

by
Linda GOYETTE

The Love Between Them

Sidney and Doreen Pittman searched for one another for the first half of their lives, looking into the eyes of strangers, hoping for tenderness. They didn't find love in a hurry.

"I had been looking for her for quite a few years before I found her," Sid explains to me. "I looked for a nice-looking person, and that is what she is."

"That's a nice compliment, Sid," Doreen murmurs, without looking up. She bends over her drawing, sharing her crayons with three-year-old Tanner who sits beside her at the kitchen table. Doreen is smiling to herself, perhaps at a memory.

Their romance began like a Saturday night movie but it deepened into something rare and valuable. They met on an exciting flight to Mexico. They knew they were in love before they returned to Canada a week later. They kept one another company for two years, with two hearts overflowing, imagining the possibility of happiness. He waited for her phone calls. She listened for his knock on the door. He proposed. She accepted. They married in a dream of a wedding at the front of a beautiful cathedral. She wore an ivory-colored dress with flowers in her hair. He wore a tuxedo and a smile as wide and warm as the sun. They had one honeymoon in a big hotel, and through the years, a second honeymoon, a third honeymoon and a fourth honeymoon on ocean cruises from the Caribbean to Alaska.

They created a home together, and eventually, a family. A decade later, they still glance at one another with a kindness that seems fresh and new.

"She is a nice girl," Sid begins. "Friendly."

"He is cute," says Doreen. "He's a nice person. He gets along well with friends. He helps me in my life."

Here is a love story, their gift to you.

"What do you want people to know about you," I asked them one afternoon.

"Write down that I've been working all my life," said Sid. "Tell them about the bike. Tell them I like living here because of the three kids, and Ron and Sheelah."

"Say that I like the kids, too," said Doreen. "I like them a lot."

They glance into the notebook as I write, watching their words flow across pages.

Sid is pushing cardboard boxes into a compacting machine in the warehouse of the Canadian Tire store in St. Albert on a Wednesday morning. This noisy machine is his responsibility. "I am really good at working with my hands," he says above the din. "I also put together the wheelbarrows, lawn mowers and bicycles." He can point to the proper location of each piece of merchandise in the warehouse, from hockey sticks to garden furniture, and he greets employees by name as he loads empty boxes into his giant wagon. "You want me to lift that for you, Sandra?" he asks. "No, I've got it, Sid," his co-worker replies. He keeps his own tool box high up on a safe shelf. Sid trained to work in the warehouse for a few months, and then, on one of the happiest days of his life, the former manager Terry Douglas called him to the front office. "Terry was a good man because he hired me," he remembers. "He asked me if I'd like to work Monday to Thursdays, regular, for $8 an hour. I said okay!"

Sid is sixty-five, a soft-spoken man who wears his red company shirt with pleasure, with a pouch of Amphora pipe tobacco tucked into his vest pocket. Born in Manitoba, he moved with his parents, brother and sister to rural Alberta as a child. "I was a little too old for the class so they took me out of school," he remembers. While young he lived as a resident at Michener Centre in Red Deer where he learned how to be a farm hand.

Later he worked on a dairy farm in Spirit River, and on a railway crew near Tofield, before he found a job as a hired hand on a farm near Legal. One day a fourteen-year-old boy, Ron de Champlain, came to visit his friend at the farm, and met Sid for the first time outside his trailer near the pig barn. In the future they would be part of the same family, but neither man nor boy knew it then.

Sid will never forget a terrible fire, sparked by an electrical short in a fan, which burned down the barn and killed hundreds of livestock. That fire upset him deeply, and changed his life. A support worker named Janet suggested he take a big trip to Mexico with a group of Albertans. He met Doreen on the plane. "We had lots to talk about that day," he says. They walked around open-air markets, and agreed they didn't like the flies that hovered over the food. They did like the same music: Wilf Carter, Webb Pierce, Hank Williams and Elvis. Sid laughed at Doreen's jokes. They looked into one another's eyes, and felt right at home.

When they returned from Mexico, Sid would take the Greyhound bus into the city every weekend to visit Doreen. "I got her an engagement ring in a short time," he says. Surrounded by family and friends, they were married on September 17, 1993. After their wedding they lived on their own in a small house in Legal, working together part-time as cleaners at their church. Ron de Champlain, by now a young support worker, and his future wife Sheelah, began visiting them three times a week. The four adults got along so well that they decided to live in the same house, so that Doreen and Sid could have independence and support. The two couples moved together to their first small home in St. Albert in 2000, along with baby Emily, but it became crowded with the arrival of the de Champlains' sons, Nicholas and Tanner. After a long search they found a larger, more comfortable home to share in a new subdivision.

They are a family—a strong circle of seven—and everyone has enough space to feel good. Sid and Doreen live in an attractive apartment of their own on the lower level of the house; Sheelah and Ron and the three children have bedrooms and a little extra family space on the top floor. All seven share meals, and enjoy one another's company throughout the day, on the main floor in between their private spaces.

Sid and Doreen have decorated their place with Sid's large paintings of their holiday cruise ships, Doreen's collection of stuffed animals and dolls, bowling trophies and family photographs. Sid stores his three guitars under the bed. Upstairs and downstairs they help the children as much as they can, looking at books, sharing snacks, and comforting them when they're hurt. "The kids call us Papa and Mama," Sid says. He and Doreen always wanted kids of their own, but long ago he had an operation at

Michener Centre which made that dream impossible. It means a lot to him to live with children who love him. "Everything is just right. Life is pretty good."

Sid rides his bicycle to Canadian Tire if the weather is good. When his old bike broke down in November, the staff decided to buy him a brand, new model. Sid appreciated the offer, but he told co-workers he could buy his own bike. "I have a job," he says. "I can afford it." He has ordered a heavy-duty, three-wheel bike, appropriately called a Workman, and he can't wait to show it to them.

Sitting in the store's lunch room, Sid talked about his toughest day on the job, the day he found out Terry Douglas had been killed in a plane crash. "It was worse for me than some other people, because he had hired me," he says. "I had to see a grief counselor." With help, he prepared a short, comforting message for everyone at the store: "I was very emotional and in tears all day," he said in the letter. "Many of the other staff members were upset as well. I asked Jay if we could put the flag at half-mast and we did." He ended the message: "There are a lot of good memories. I will miss Terry and always remember him."

He went home to Doreen that afternoon, as always. She can make him feel better like nobody else.

"Married people should try to get along," Sid says. "We get in arguments sometimes but we make up for it."

Doreen loves riddles. "What three keys can't open a door?" she asks, pausing for a guess. "Give up? A donkey, a turkey and a monkey!"

Two days a week Doreen takes the Handi-Bus to the St. Albert Senior Citizens Club. Today she is sitting at a long table with her friends, placing bits of coloured tissue paper on a design to make a brilliant flower. She excuses herself and offers me a tour of the centre, around the people at the bridge tables, past the cook and the dishwashers in the kitchen, around the billiard tables, past the pedicure lady and into the craft shop. Everyone greets her by name.

"I like to help," she says later, as we sit with our coffee. "I like to show people where to put their coats if they are new here, and help them find the bathroom. We talk about things, do crossword puzzles, and do arts and crafts." She is sixty-two, a neatly-dressed woman with soft, grey hair and a friendly smile. She shows me a blue and purple wristwatch, a recent birthday gift from her husband. "Sid took me out to a restaurant for my birthday and they gave us bullhorn hats to wear. He was trying to get the camera together, and I was trying to hold the hat on my head!"

Doreen has a good memory for other people's birthdays, something they like about her. She grew up in Edmonton's west end, the youngest daughter in a family of five children. As a little girl she attended Winnifred Stewart School where she learned how to read. Her favourite books are riddle books. "Sometimes I have trouble with spelling but I keep at it. I can do my times tables. I can add and take away, but I can't divide." She lived with her mother for many years, and later moved to a group home. There she met her first boyfriend. He wasn't the man she wanted to marry, so she kept looking. Doreen worked for a long time as a table cleaner at Pizza Hut, but she prefers her quiet afternoons at the seniors' club. "I like the whole works. I like everybody in here. They are all polite. They are all good friends to me."

She and Sid have learned a lot about marriage over the years. "We have to get away from each other sometimes," she says. This summer Sid will go horse-back riding at the Circle Square Ranch and the Black Cat Guest Ranch and go fishing with his brother, Richard. While he is away Doreen plans to learn how to knit and how to cook something besides scrambled eggs and grilled cheese sandwiches. She will also fly to Nanaimo to visit two of her sisters. Sheelah will come along for the fun. After a holiday apart, or a day in different places, Doreen and Sid return home with something interesting to tell one other. Sid might talk about his Knights of Columbus meeting. Doreen might show him the door prize she won, or tell him about the funny cartoon she watched with the kids. They enjoy their time together more if they have a little breathing room. On Fridays they go together to the LOSECA community centre to meet friends. On Saturdays they go bowling. On Sundays they go to church. "I like to dance with Sid, too," says Doreen, adding that the music has to be right to put them in the mood. "Sid and I don't care for rock and roll."

They have their differences, like any couple, she says. "Sid snores," she confided one evening. Sid looked up, one eyebrow raised. "You snore, too, Doreen." Then Doreen said she disapproved of Sid's pipe smoking. Then Sid said he disapproves when Doreen wakes him for church at seven a.m. Do they have a secret for staying happy? "Oh, brother, that," says Doreen, thinking about the question. "Try to get along okay. No fighting. No divorce. You can have little break-ups, but not too many."

Patience is an important part of Doreen's nature. The children often turn to her if they want an extra-long game of Xs and Os, or if they want to put together the same jigsaw puzzle more than once. They know they can curl up in the warm curve of her arm to watch a favourite movie for the fourth time. When Nicholas and Tanner were babies, napping in the afternoon, Doreen entertained Emily to give their young mother a rest. One day the little girl climbed the stairs, holding Doreen's slipper as if it were made of gold. "I can tie a bow!" she told her mother. Slowly and carefully, she wound laces around loops with Doreen coaching her gently from the sidelines: "Keep going, Emily! You're doing great!" A slipper soon had a wobbly bow. Now that Emily is six-years-old, Doreen likes to remind her how she learned to tie her shoes when she was only three.

"I want to say I am happy, not sad," says Doreen, talking into the notebook again. She counts blessings on her fingertips: Tanner, Nicholas and Emily, her brothers and sisters, her nieces and nephews, "and I have Ron and Sheelah, and I have Sid." She touches his gift on her wrist, rolling up the arm of her sweater so people will be sure to see how beautiful it is. Soon it will be time to go home to him. "What bow is impossible to tie?" she asks. "Give up? A rainbow!"

The sign at the entrance of the St. Albert Bowling Centre says: "The Finest People in the World Walk Through These Doors—Our Customers." Inside, Sid and Doreen are waiting for their turn under the score monitors. Doreen makes frequent trips to the snack bar for juice, pop and chocolate bars, but she keeps her eye on her teammates, especially the handsome one. "Your turn, Sid! Come on, now, you can do it!" Sid gets a strike. Doreen claps her hands. She takes her turn. "I made another spare, Sid!" When she is upset about her score, he touches her hand to calm her. She hands him a tissue so he can wipe his eyeglasses, and see the pins better.

When the game ends, the coach and the other teammates say goodbye until next Saturday. Sid bends down and unties each of Doreen's bowling shoes. He helps her on with her winter boots. "Thanks, Sid," she says. He packs their bowling bag, and lifts it to his shoulder. "Let's go, Doreen," he says. She takes his arm to go home.

Tonight they will sleep beside one another, with love in the darkness between them, knowing what the morning will bring.

by
Debbie MARSHALL

Away from the Edge

It is a scorching hot day in July 2006 and I am on my way to meet 24-year-old Danielle Husak, a young woman living in Sherwood Park, a small community just north of Edmonton. Her mother, Cheryl Adam, has already sent me an email describing her daughter's early years. According to Cheryl, Danielle was "home schooled as she became increasingly violent and had outbursts that the school system could not cope with...she was integrated back into the school system completing her Grade 12 at Jasper Place High School...during her school years, Danielle played community soccer, rugby, skied, and completed her swimming lessons...she will be entering a graphic design course at Norquest in the fall..."

Except for the violent outbursts, Danielle's life sounds remarkably like that of my own daughter—a girl who enjoyed the usual daydreams, music lessons, and hot summers spent at camp, a teenager who rolled her eyes when asked to do chores, loved retro-rock and knew how to push all her parents' buttons. But I knew that Danielle's childhood was very different from that of my daughter; beneath Cheryl's cheerful e-words lay a life of struggle, of trying to draw her daughter away from the edge of a mental and emotional chasm.

The Starbucks on Baseline Road is remarkably quiet. There is only one table at which an obvious mother-daughter combination is seated. Cheryl Adam looks right into my eyes and gives me a frank smile, the kind that says "I am who I am, take me or leave me." She is average height, with reddish-brown hair, comfortably dressed in a white t-shirt and jeans. I apologize for being late (not a good start) and she introduces me to Danielle. This poised, serious looking young woman with the fashionably narrow glasses and shy sidelong glance is not at all who I expect. Where is the violent girl described in the email?

We begin with the usual small-talk, questions about Danielle's plans for college and her new job at the Mercantile, a funky independent grocery store. But soon we are traveling backward in time. Cheryl does most of the talking, while Danielle sits quietly, nodding vigorously or looking down into her coffee cup when the recollections are painful.

I learn that when Danielle was born in 1982, Cheryl Adam and Dan Husak were young parents and their new baby was more than the usual handful. According to Cheryl, Danielle was a "colicky" infant who was awake twenty-three hours out of every twenty-four. It quickly became apparent that she was unusual, an infant who wouldn't respond when her name was called, or look directly into her mother's eyes. "She wasn't engaging with people and wouldn't answer when you called her name," says Cheryl. She wondered if Danielle was deaf. She wasn't, but Danielle *was* aggressive, throwing fierce tantrums while still in the crib.

At first, Cheryl blamed herself for her daughter's behaviour. "You doubt yourself as a parent," she says. But a few years later, after giving birth to her second daughter Michelle, Cheryl realized that Danielle's behaviours went way beyond the normal range expressed by children of her own age. Unlike Danielle, Michelle was a calm, happy baby who slept well, made visual connections with her mother, and seldom lost her temper.

For a while, the young parents rationalized away the differences between their daughters. After all, siblings often have very different personalities. When Cheryl went back to school to become a respiratory therapist, both girls were placed in daycare. Danielle soon graduated to kindergarten and it was at this point that her ability to cope with the outside world began to show signs of strain. Kindergarten was a noisy place. Children were encouraged to play at various activity stations. Each of these offered a different play option—from playing house to building sand castles. For Danielle, it was overwhelming. She became disruptive, throwing increasingly noisy tantrums and hitting other children. Her parents were asked to remove her from kindergarten. Cheryl sought answers, taking Danielle to their family doctor and on to a pediatrician. But according to the medical professionals, Danielle was "perfectly fine."

Cheryl wondered if the school system was the source of the problem and opted to place her daughter in an expensive, highly structured Montessori school. For a while, Danielle thrived and her tantrums settled down. All that changed when it was time to enroll her in public school. After just a few days, Danielle's grade one teacher informed Cheryl that her daughter had serious learning problems.

Defensive, Cheryl questioned how the teacher could make such a sweeping assessment after spending such a short time with her child. Yet deep inside, she had to admit the truth. Something *was* wrong with Danielle. But what? More visits to more doctors led to mistaken diagnoses. Danielle's problems, one doctor claimed, were the result of allergies to both the hydrocortisone crème used to treat her eczema and to a whole host of foods. Cheryl put her daughter onto a special diet and sent her back to school. Together, she and Danielle's teacher persevered for the rest of the school year.

Everything seemed fine until Danielle turned eight. She was still having violent tantrums, however, her parents were able to control her and the diet seemed to help. "Then everything melted down," remembers Cheryl. She had given Danielle a "time-out" for aggressive behaviour. Danielle used the opportunity to slip out of the house and run away. A frantic Cheryl called the police. Danielle was finally found, having locked herself in the trunk of an unused old car that the family kept in the garage. Grateful to find Danielle safe, but by now desperate to know what was troubling her, Cheryl and Dan checked their daughter into the psychiatric ward at the University of Alberta Hospital. "We wanted an answer," says Cheryl.

Hospital psychiatrists diagnosed Danielle as having Attention Deficit Hyperactivity Disorder (ADHD) with a Central Auditory Processing Defect (CAPD). "[People with this disorder] can't screen out sounds or focus on one sound or on one person talking," says Cheryl. Although they would soon learn that the diagnosis was less than complete, for a time, it seemed to make sense. Danielle was placed on medications and the family went into a relative period of calm.

That calm was shattered soon after Danielle turned twelve. At that time, her psychiatrist recommended that Danielle take a "drug holiday." Medications sometimes lose their efficacy if taken for too long, so he reasoned that Danielle should be switched to some other drugs for a while. Unfortunately, the change in medication brought back some of Danielle's most nightmarish symptoms. On Valentine's Day 1994, Cheryl got a call from her daughter's school principal. Danielle had beaten up children (including her own sister) on the school bus that morning. The violence hadn't ended there. When she was brought into the school office, Danielle ripped it apart, throwing and breaking whatever she could reach. School officials called an ambulance and Danielle was taken to the University of Alberta Hospital.

"They admitted her and did a ton of tests," remembers Cheryl. "MRIs, CTs and stuff like that that to figure out what the deal was." Since there were no beds in the psychiatric ward, Danielle was admitted to a regular ward, watched over by two security guards. When she trashed the room, everything was removed but her bed. Soon a space was found in the psychiatric ward and Danielle spent the next few months being assessed.

The hospital was an isolating, frightening place, says Danielle. "There was a 'time-out room.' If you'd had a bad day, they'd throw a mattress in there with a blanket and leave me there!" Danielle frowns as her mother describes how a hospital psychiatrist recommended that she institutionalize her daughter. "He said that she would never improve," remembers Cheryl.

That was a verdict that the Husak's were unwilling to accept. After removing Danielle from the hospital, Cheryl took her to another psychiatrist. He concluded that Danielle had a mild form of "pervasive developmental disorder." When she went to the medical library to find out what this meant, Cheryl was devastated. Danielle was autistic. "[A decade ago], autism was a *bad* diagnosis," says Cheryl. Autistic children are like hyper-sensitive radar systems. They pick up all the sounds and activities going on around them and find it almost impossible to screen out the world's noise. Terribly over-stimulated, they have great difficulty focusing and making sense of the world around them. They become tremendously frustrated and often have behavioural problems. In 1994, there were very few treatments for the disorder and parents of autistic children often felt isolated and abandoned.

Cheryl decided to take Danielle's future into her own hands. She quit her job as a respiratory therapist and decided to home school her. Along the way, Cheryl enlisted the help of many local professionals. "It took a whole village to raise Danielle," she says.

"Who was in that village?" I ask Danielle.

She smiles and names her mother first, than lists a whole series of pediatricians, child psychologists, teaching assistants, aides and community support workers, a veritable who's who of Edmonton's medical and social work professionals. Among these names is one that particularly stands out for Danielle—Kris Knudson, a family aide who came to work for the Husak's when she was ten-years-old. I interview Kris later, by phone. He remembers the first time he met Danielle. "I came into the kitchen and Cheryl and Michelle were sitting at the kitchen table. Danielle was in the middle of the kitchen floor, hiding under a blanket."

As he got to know Danielle, Kris discovered that she saw the world in two-dimensional terms. Everything had to be concrete, "she had to exist in black and white, no gray," says Knudson. If her day didn't go exactly as planned, from milk being in the refrigerator when she came down for breakfast to trips to the swimming pool happening exactly at the time planned, Danielle would "lose it—throw things, scream."

Cheryl called in a specialist who prescribed a behaviour-modification program for Danielle. This quote, taken from the specialist's report, outlines in cool tones the extent of the challenges faced by her family:

The daily frequency of aggressive behavior was recorded throughout April 8 to April 20/94. This information indicates that Danielle averages nine aggressions a day. Aggressions primarily occur throughout school hours.

Danielle's "aggressions" included kicking, punching, biting, throwing objects, scratching, spitting and throwing herself on the floor. The plan recommended that Cheryl analyze her eldest daughter's behaviour every fifteen minutes throughout the day and place a smiley-face sticker on a special chart each time she acted appropriately. If Danielle acted aggressively, she received an "x." The more stickers that she earned, the more treats—hockey cards, comic books, baseball tickets—she would receive.

Kris Knudson helped Cheryl put this regime into practice. He arrived each morning around eight o'clock. He and Cheryl would have coffee until Danielle made her way into the kitchen for breakfast. Then "school" would begin. "We tried to keep her on task with as much of the regular Alberta curriculum as we could," says Kris. "We'd go through different units. There'd be lots of aggressions [by Danielle], time-outs, sometimes ten or fifteen in a morning. When she was frustrated, she'd push her foot on top of the other foot so hard she'd rub the skin off. She would yell, scream, throw things. There were no coping mechanisms for her to deal with her frustrations." During some of her "aggressions," Kris and Cheryl would have to hold Danielle down while she kicked, spit, and head-butted anyone in her vicinity.

There weren't many stickers on the chart at the end of most days. Yet there were also moments when another Danielle appeared. "Danielle always had a part of her—you'd see flashes of it—when she was absolutely an innocent, sweet little girl who wanted to be accepted by the world," says Kris. Remarkably, as time passed, that sweet little girl began to appear for longer periods of time. At thirteen, Danielle was able to join a local girls' soccer team. Now Cheryl observed a new challenge. Danielle didn't seem able to make friends.

Autistic children are often indifferent to those around them. They don't make eye contact and sometimes have difficulty "reading" other people. Danielle seemed unable to recognize and comprehend the subtle cues that help most people understand what others are saying to them. What's more, she didn't seem to know how to reach out to others and build relationships. "As a grade six and seven student, she felt really alone," remembers Kris Knudson.

While Cheryl couldn't make friends for Danielle, she could help her daughter develop relationship skills. Danielle was enrolled in a program at the Glenrose Hospital in which she was taught how to make eye contact. She also began to participate in programs offered by Chrysalis, a local agency dedicated to people who have developmental disabilities. Danielle, now passionate about sports, participated in the Special Olympics. She also went to a special summer camp sponsored by Chrysalis. There she made her first best friends.

Being with other young persons with disabilities remains important to Danielle. "They're on the same level playing field as me—they're disabled too," says Danielle. "I can read their emotions. Non-disabled people hold back their emotions." Unfortunately, the acceptance Danielle experienced at camp and at Special Olympics wasn't always present in other arenas of her adolescent life. "I was on a rugby team with non-disabled kids for three years. I never missed a practice but I never got to play in one game," says Danielle. "[My coach] didn't think I was good enough. She had a reputation to maintain."

As the years passed, Danielle slowly settled down. There were fewer and fewer tantrums. Cheryl isn't sure if this was the result of the hard work that she and Kris had been doing or simply the by-product of the natural process of maturity. Whatever the reason, by the time she was eighteen, Danielle was able to control her behaviour to the point that Cheryl decided to enroll her in a normal grade twelve program at a local high school.

Things were finally looking up for Danielle. She was studying among her own peers, even holding down a part time job at a local restaurant. Unfortunately, during this hiatus, the rest of the family began to crash. The stress of raising Danielle had taken its toll on everyone. Cheryl and Dan had divorced, their marriage fractured from the strain of caring for a violent child. Cheryl had developed chronic insomnia, a condition that had begun years earlier when Danielle had threatened to kill her mother as she slept. Michelle Husak had become withdrawn and introspective, her own needs often lost in the family's struggle to keep Danielle on track. She had also been the victim of some of Danielle's rages. "I wasn't always nice to my sister," says Danielle.

Burned out and emotionally spent, Cheryl had a breakdown. "I couldn't look at Danielle and not see work—I was exhausted," she says. Cheryl took her own "time-out," leaving Danielle and Michelle in the care of Kris Knudson. After a short time, Cheryl managed to bring the shattered pieces of herself back together. She eventually sold her home and moved to the country. Within two years, both her daughters were living with her once again.

Today, the wounds have healed, and there is a greater calm surrounding Cheryl and her two daughters. A settled, happier Danielle is beginning to embrace life on her own terms. She will soon be starting her new job at the Mercantile and is ready for a whole new set of responsibilities. "With this new job, I'll be biking twice a week," she says. "Mum could drive me but that doesn't teach me anything." In the fall, Danielle will begin the graphic design program at Norquest College. "I like creating things," she says.

Danielle's long term goal is to get a well-paying job and live independently. For her, that means living alone. While she has learned to socialize and has built some important friendships, she values her privacy and enjoys her own company. "I want a place of my own," says Danielle. "I have a few friends from Special Olympics who'd like to live with me, but I'm sorry, I don't want to be their mum. I want an apartment of my own."

That hunger for solitude extends to her romantic relationships. "I don't want to get married. I want to be responsible for myself," Danielle says simply. This is hard for her mother to accept. Like many parents, Cheryl dreamed of her daughter settling down and having a family. However, she has come to terms with Danielle's approach to life. "It's not a common path," says Cheryl, "but it's her path."

Whatever Danielle may accomplish in her life, she has achieved some great things without realizing it. Kris Knudson was transformed by his experience with her. "Working with Cheryl, Michelle, and Danielle, I had a chance to walk with wounded people. There's something about walking that road with them that taught me about being human. We all bear scars and wounds." Kris went on to work with street people, drug addicts, and prostitutes, eventually become a pastor at Edmonton's inner-city Mustard Seed outreach centre.

Arguably the person whose life has been most affected by Danielle is her mother. Raising Danielle has affected the way in which Cheryl approaches the work that she does each day. "I have more compassion for the clients I serve in my work as a respiratory therapist," she says. Accustomed to having others intervening in her own family's life, she has become especially sensitive when entering the lives of those who need her services.

Just as she once learned to celebrate the smallest amount of progress in her daughter, Cheryl has also learned to see the joy in the small things of everyday life and the importance of relationships and family. "I think if I had not had the experience [of raising Danielle] I would have just plodded through my life," says Cheryl. "Without that experience I don't think I would have been as close to my girls as I am. And I might not have realized that my children are not an extension of who I am. They are separate human beings. They have achieved great things, but their achievements are their own."

As I rise to leave the coffee shop, I shake hands with Cheryl and then with Danielle. This time, she looks me right in the eyes and smiles. It's a small act, but it was once impossible, and it is the best sign that Danielle is making a successful life, away from the edge.

Contributors

Todd Babiak

Todd Babiak is a reporter for the *Edmonton Journal*, writing for the Culture section and for *ed magazine*. He is also the author of the novels *Choke Hold* and *The Garneau Block*. *The Garneau Block* was first serialized in the *Journal*. His third novel, *The Book of Stanley*, will be serialized in September 2006.

Heather Boyd

Heather Boyd works with The Canadian Press news service. She's the proud mother of three sons. Her father was a forensic psychiatrist who worked for institutions in Hamilton and Penetanguishene, Ont. "Our family lived on the hospital grounds and I pretty much spent my childhood growing up with people like Carol Ann," says Heather.

Jackie Boyko

Jackie Boyko is an Edmonton-based freelance graphic designer. She attended both the University of Alberta and the Northern Alberta Institute of Technology (NAIT) specializing in both art and graphic communications. Before starting her own business (Credo Young Enterprises) four years ago, she worked for numerous firms throughout the city. Her work has been featured in many magazines including her award-winning "Survivor" communications package in the 2002 edition of *Dynamic Graphics*.

Allan Chambers

Allan Chambers is an Edmonton-based freelance writer and journalist. He worked for the *Edmonton Journal* for many years, and for several newspapers in eastern Canada. His work appears in numerous magazines. "Every story teaches you something," he says. "I went to the Nina Haggerty Centre for the Arts to interview Leona Clawson and came away with renewed respect for work that is done for its own sake. You couldn't separate the artists from their work. They were in wonderful harmony with their space and their materials. I made up excuses to go back a couple of times. I wanted to be in that atmosphere where everything fell away except for what was being created."

Allan also profiled Blaze Logan. "Blaze looks at the world through eyes that are trusting and accepting. He seems to find everything fascinating. I wanted to take a lesson from that."

Yvonne DuBourdieu

Yvonne DuBourdieu photographed the people profiled in *Big Enough Dreams* and has produced and directed a film based on some of the stories in the book. Yvonne began her career as a producer and director in Glasgow, Scotland where she worked on documentary and educational films for Channel 4 Television, Scottish Television, and independent production companies. Since moving to Canada, she has worked as a producer/director for Access Network and CBC-TV where she garnered numerous awards for commercials, PSAs, and educational films. She has her own independent production company, Arthouse Productions. Yvonne also directed and produced the film *Through the Eyes of Artists*. It offers a rare and magical glimpse into the world of a group of artists with developmental disabilities.

Caterina Edwards

Caterina Edwards' book *The Island of the Nightingales* won the 2000 Writers Guild of Alberta Award for Short Fiction. She has also published a novel, a book of novellas, and a play, as well as numerous essays and short stories in literary magazines and anthologies. Caterina is particularly proud of the two books of life writing by women that she co-edited. Recently, she completed both a final draft of a novel and a work of creative non-fiction about caring for her mother, who suffered from dementia.

"Working on this article about Lindsay Biehn was a revelation. In my first novel *The Lion's Mouth*, one of the main characters has a Down syndrome child, but that father allows the difficulties to embitter him. He and his wife overprotect the child so that the boy has no agency and no measure of independence. Getting to know Lindsay and her family exposed me to the opposite response. The Biehns have found the right balance between help and empowerment."

Curtis Gillespie

Curtis Gillespie has written three books and numerous magazine articles. He lives in Edmonton with his wife and two daughters.

"I worked in the social services for many years before becoming a writer, and I still volunteer in the field," says Curtis. "The one thing that has never ceased to inspire and amaze me—and this was certainly the case with Greg—is the unfailing optimism of the people we serve in the field. It's a lesson most of us could benefit from learning."

Linda Goyette

Edmonton writer Linda Goyette recently edited the anthology, *Standing Together*. She is also the author of *Edmonton In Our Own Words*, which won the 2005 Grant MacEwan Author's Award; *Kidmonton*, a companion volume for children; and *Second Opinion*, a collection of her newspaper columns. Linda enjoyed the hours she spent with Doreen and Sid Pittman, and the deChamplain family. "It was pure pleasure to write about their love for one another, and to laugh with them," says Linda. "Do you know the kind of people who make you cheerful, just to be around them? They have found the secret of a happy life—love somebody."

Mark Haroun

Mark Haroun is an Edmonton playwright and recent graduate of the University of Alberta. *A Giraffe in Paris*, Mark's play for young audiences, received its premiere at the Citadel Theatre and received the 2005 Elizabeth Sterling Haynes award for best production for young audiences.

"Getting to know Brent Hickey was a tremendous experience," says Mark. "I am inspired by Brent's determination and touched by his heart, which he wears proudly on his sleeve."

Gary Holdgrafer

Gary Holdgrafer is a Professor Emeritus at the University of Alberta in Speech-Language Pathology. He also works with his partner Mary in a number of pursuits that include creativity coaching and teaching courses on personal learning. He has written scholarly articles as well as creative non-fiction and children's fiction.

"Contributing to this anthology about persons with developmental disabilities was a very impacting personal learning experience," says Gary. "I challenged myself to be continually aware of my impressions and to probe until I was satisfied that I was telling her story and not one I made up about her."

Kalin Jensen

Kalin Jensen is a recent graduate from the University of Alberta with a major in English and minor in Creative Writing. "I didn't know what to expect when I signed on for this project," says Kalin. "But I came out of it with a greater understanding of how Down syndrome not only affects the individual who has the disability, but everyone associated with that person as well. Christian is so charming, funny, and well-adjusted that I hope we cross paths again." Kalin also profiled Michelle Arklie.

Myrna Kostash

Myrna Kostash is a full time writer living in Edmonton, Alberta. She is author of *Baba's Children* (1978); *Long Way From Home: The Story of the Sixties Generation in Canada* (1980); *No Kidding: Inside the World of Teenage Girls* (1987); *Bloodlines: A Journey Into Eastern Europe* (1993); *The Doomed Bridegroom: A Memoir* (1997); *The Next Canada: Looking for the Future Nation* (2000); *Reading the River: A Traveller's Companion to the North Saskatchewan River* (2005). *My Demetrius* is a work-in-progress.

Besides writing for diverse magazines, from *Chatelaine* to *Saturday Night* to *Border Crossings*, to *Canadian Geographic*, Myrna has written radio drama and documentary, television documentary, and theatre cabaret. Her creative non-fiction has appeared in *Brick, Border Crossings, Descant, The Camrose Review, Capilano Review, Prairie Fire, Geist, dandeLion, CV II, Literatura na swiecie* (Warsaw), *Stozher* (Skopje), and *Mostovi* (Belgrade). Her essays and articles have appeared in numerous anthologies.

"Thinking about my relationship with Jocelyn Bell has underscored for me how much 'community' I do in fact share with people with disabilities," says Myrna. "They do not live on another planet, they are my neighbours. Talk about diversity!"

Mark Kozub

Mark Kozub is a freelance magazine writer, founder of Edmonton's Raving Poets, and author of the coffee table book, *A Calgary Album: Glimpses of the Way We Were* (Hounslow Press). In 2006, Dramatic Situations published Kozub's debut novel *The Brown Family*, a bittersweet comedy that Vue Weekly's Carolyn Nikodym says "blurs the line between ordinary and extraordinary."

Mark says that meeting Dan Atkinson was a memorable experience. "For starters, doing this piece made me realize that we all have our prejudices. Or at the very least we like to put people in boxes. Driving over to Dan's home on a very cold and VERY snowy day, I really didn't know what to expect. I hadn't met the man yet. All I knew was that he had a disability. When I came to his doorstep, though, he opened the door and I immediately felt his warmth. He was a good and slightly excited host, entertaining and disarmingly honest. And he was quirky too. We all have our quirks, don't we? It's what makes us human. And interesting. And Dan is both."

Allison Kydd

Allison Kydd is amazed by the variety of people she meets in her role as a freelance writer. Each new project introduces new worlds and, more important, offers new insights into human nature. When asked to take part in this project, she wondered whether she was equal to the challenge. What in her previous experience as a writer whose first love is fiction, a journalist who has focused on Aboriginal issues, classical music and religious issues, qualified her for this task?

"When I met Les Murrell, I was reminded that this project wasn't about me. Leslie has more than enough ideas, more than enough stories to tell," says Allison. "In spite of some tough experiences such as living on the street, he has kept his dreams of being an actor and comedian. I didn't have to work hard to 'draw out my subject.' Instead, my biggest challenge was just trying to keep up with him."

Sophie Lees

Sophie Lees is an award-winning freelance writer, whose works have appeared in magazines such as *AlbertaViews, Alberta Venture, Avenue, and Utne*. While working on this project, Lees's father had a massive stroke and Ann's story took on an even deeper significance. "Brain injury just wasn't a topic I'd thought about before," Lees said. "But knowing how much Ann has accomplished gives me hope for my father's recovery. Instead of focusing on the abilities he's lost, I think about the abilities he does have and will have. It's a different way of looking at life, one that Ann helped me see."

Beverly MacKinnon

Beverly MacKinnon was born and raised in Collingwood, Ontario and moved Edmonton, Alberta in 1980. In 1986 she met and married Bill MacKinnon and established a home in the West. For seven years Beverly was employed in the manual labour workforce. This changed in 1987, when an accident made physical work impossible.

In 1989, Beverly gave birth to her daughter Sarah. Sarah was born with learning disabilities. Beverly decided that, in order to help her daughter with schoolwork, she needed to upgrade her reading and writing skills.

In 1993, Beverly's doctor told her about Project Adult Literacy Society (P.A.L.S.). PALS introduced her to other adult literacy programs. Each program helped her reach her goals and make new ones. She can now read at a grade five level and enjoys writing as well. "I am much more sure of myself and hope to one day be a teachers aide," says Beverly. "Through my activity at the [Adult Literacy] Learning Center I am trying to let other adults, like myself, know that there is help for them also." In 2005, Beverly won the Canada Post Literacy award for Alberta.

"To have my story in this publication makes me feel happy and honoured once again," says Beverly. "I believe that my success will help others by showing them that with hard work and determination, they too will succeed."

Cheryl Mahaffy

Cheryl Mahaffy is co-author of *Agora Borealis*, an exploration of sustainable building design. Her writing also appears in periodicals and in two anthologies published in 2005: *Edmonton on Location* and *Outside of Ordinary*. Current projects include *100 Journeys*, to be published by the Alberta Motor Association later in 2006 and *Women Building Alberta*, which profiles early women architects. Mother of three, she lives in Edmonton with husband Peter and works with numerous clients under the moniker *Words that Sing*.

"Writing this profile of John Benes earned me a spot on his list of annual lunch partners," says Cheryl. "I'm looking forward to our next meal together, particularly since I don't smoke."

Alice Major

Alice Major, Edmonton's first poet laureate, has lived in that city since 1981. She emigrated from Scotland at the age of eight, and grew up in Toronto before coming west to work as a weekly newspaper reporter in British Columbia. She has published six poetry collections, and a new collection, *The Occupied World*, will be published by the University of Alberta Press later this year.

Alice has been active in the writing community for two decades. She is past president of the Writers Guild of Alberta and of the League of Canadian Poets. And she was the second chair of the Edmonton Arts Council. She was appointed the city's first Poet Laureate in June, 2005.

Debbie Marshall

Debbie Marshall is an Alberta writer and editor. She is the co-editor of *Spiritual Quest: Stories from Life* (UCPH: 2003), the co-author of *Candles to Kilowatts: The Story of Edmonton's Power Company* (Duval House: 2002), and is the author of the forthcoming biography *Give Your Other Vote to the Sister: A Woman's Journey into the Great War* (University of Calgary Press: 2007). Her articles and essays have appeared in numerous local and national magazines and anthologies.

Heather Marshall

Heather Marshall is an Edmonton-area writer and editor. In addition to contributing to several Alberta magazines, she is the co-author of *Candles to Kilowatts: The Story of Edmonton's Power Company* (Duval House: 2002). She has edited many books, including *By Degrees: The First 90 Years of the Canadian Federation of University Women Edmonton* (CFUWE: 2004). Heather is also the former publisher of Rowan Books, an Edmonton-based poetry press.

"Writing about Matthew reminded me of the in-between place that many people with developmental disabilities find themselves in," says Heather. "They are often aware of their limits and get frustrated by them. Matthew seems to be finding ways to deal with the obstacles in his path and is making the best of his life."

Gary McPherson

In June of 1998, Gary McPherson became the Executive Director of the Canadian Centre for Social Entrepreneurship (CCSE) in the School of Business at the University of Alberta. He is also an Adjunct Professor, as well as a Special Lecturer and Advisor in the Faculty of Physical Education and Recreation. Prior to joining the University, Gary served for ten years as Chairman of the Alberta Premier's Council on the Status of Persons with Disabilities. In 2000, he authored and self-published *With Every Breath I Take*, a book about personal health and responsibility. Canmore author Gerald Hankins has written a biography of Gary entitled *Rolling On* (University of Alberta Press: 2003).

Gary McPherson has an Honourary Doctorate of Laws Degree from the University of Alberta and has also received the Order of Canada. He has also been selected as one of the top 100 Edmontonians of the Century.

Lorie Miseck

Lorie Miseck was born in Alberta's Peace River country. She now makes her home in Edmonton with her partner Terry, their daughters Maeve and Emily, and their two dogs. She is a poet whose books include the *blue not seen* (Rowan Books, 1997) and the award-winning a *Promise of Salt* (Coteau Books, 2002).

Michelle Ponich

Michelle Ponich is a graduate of the Journalism program at MacEwan College. Communicating through various art forms has always been a passion for her. She is a singer, dancer and actress, as well as a writer. Michelle has written about her sister Tanya for this anthology, as well as for CBC TV and Radio. "Writing about my sister brought up so many feelings and emotions it forced me to dig deep and look at her through a different set of eyes," says Michelle. "Tanya has taught me more about myself and about life than anyone else."

Dan Rubinstein

Dan is a writer and magazine editor living in Edmonton. While spending time with Jennifer, Sean, Karen and Clem Lefebvre, it struck him repeatedly that they're a family dealing with the same types of issues that all families face. "I find it chilling that Karen and Clem might not have married and had kids because of their developmental disabilities," says Dan.

Susan Ruttan

Susan Ruttan is an *Edmonton Journal* reporter. "I have been in the newspaper business for 35 years in a variety of capacities, and have been at the *Journal* since 1996," says Susan. "For me, writing the portrait of James was a challenge, because he is not very verbal so couldn't be interviewed in the normal way. I had to get to know James by talking to people who knew him and loved him, and by simply observing him closely. It was a very rewarding experience."

Gloria Sawai

Gloria Sawai is a writer, editor and teacher. Her most famous short story, "The Day I Sat with Jesus on the Sundeck and a Wind Came Up and Blew My Kimono Open and He Saw My Breasts," has appeared in many anthologies and literary journals. Her book, *A Song for Nettie Johnson*, won the Henry Kreisel Award for Best First Book (Alberta Book Awards), Danuta Gleed Award for best first collection of short stories (Writers' Union of Canada), and the 2002 Governor General's Literary Award. Her plays have been produced by Alberta Theatre Projects and the Edmonton Fringe Festival. Raised in Saskatchewan, Gloria now lives in Edmonton.

Christie Schultz

Christie Schultz is an Edmonton-based writer. In addition to writing biography and profile pieces, she writes about food and the outdoors for *Vue Weekly*. She also contributes to *Edmonton Life* magazine and her fiction has recently appeared in *Alberta Views*. Of this project and Dean Kirkby, she says, "I didn't expect to see so many similarities between me and Dean. If difference divides, recognition of similarities might be a step towards growing more supportive communities."

Shirley A. Serviss

Shirley A. Serviss is an Edmonton-based writer, editor and writing instructor. She has published three collections of poetry. Her most recent, *Hitchhiking in the Hospital* (Inkling Press: 2005), is based on over five years of experience as a poet at the University of Alberta Hospital. Her articles, poetry and essays have appeared in numerous publications and anthologies and she is co-editor of a collection of women's writing on depression entitled *Study in Grey* (Rowan Books, 1999). In addition to her hospital work, she edits *WestWord*, the magazine of the Writers Guild of Alberta and teaches writing courses for Athabasca University, University of Alberta's Faculty of Extension and MacEwan College.

"Writing this piece made me much more aware of my own disabilities— negativity, fear of taking physical risks—as I encountered Marlene's positive, daredevil attitude towards life," says Shirley.

Gayle Simonson

Gayle Simonson is an Edmonton-based freelance writer. In the past she specialized in the development of environmental education programs but now is enjoying work in a variety of subjects. Working on this project was particularly significant. She has a niece who has faced many of the same situations that Erin has encountered, so realizes the importance of recognizing the gifts that such young women can offer if given the opportunity.

"I enjoyed meeting Erin and would like to thank Erin, her mom Brenda and her case worker Marina for their cooperation," says Gayle. "It was truly a pleasure to tell Erin's story."

Davey Thompson

Davey Thompson created the cover illustration for *Big Enough Dreams*. She is an Edmonton-based illustrator. Her work has appeared in a range of publications including the *Harvard Business Review*, *Wall Street Journal* and *Maclean's*.

Debby Waldman

Debby Waldman has a journalism degree from Syracuse University and a Master of Fine Arts degree in creative writing from Cornell University. Her writing has appeared in a variety of publications, including *People Magazine, Sports Illustrated, Sports Illustrated for Kids, Chatelaine, and Publishers Weekly*. She writes a bi-weekly family/humour column as well as book reviews for the *Edmonton Journal*. She is the co-author, with audiologist Jackson Roush, of *Your Child's Hearing Loss: What Parents Need to Know*, inspired by her daughter, who is hard-of-hearing. Her children's picture book, *A Sack Full of Feathers*, was published in 2006 by Orca. She lives in Edmonton with her husband and two children.

Naturally curious—some people would call her nosy—Debby loves talking to people and learning about their lives. "I feel honoured to have been asked to contribute to this anthology, and truly enjoyed meeting Pamela, her parents, and her boss at the Wye Gardens Dairy Queen," says Debby.

Christine Wiesenthal

Christine Wiesenthal is a poet, literary critic and biographer based in Edmonton. Her latest book, *The Half-Lives of Pat Lowther* (University of Toronto Press: 2005), was recently awarded the Canadian Historical Association's Clio Prize for British Columbia.

For Christine, meeting Jan and her parents, and writing Jan's profile, was a rewarding and illuminating experience. "I felt humbled by the unassuming courage and faith I discovered in Jan, and by the fierce love she inspires in others," she says. "Writing this piece made me think not only about how much I take for granted in my own life, but about all manner of quietly exceptional lives, unfolding around us everyday, that too often go publicly unrecorded."

Acknowledgements

Big Enough Dreams is the product of many people's creative input. It is, first and foremost, the brainchild of the Edmonton Learning Community—a group of self advocates, parents, service providers, government employees, and educators interested in promoting positive images of people with developmental disabilities. The Learning Community came up with the idea for the book and fostered its development, hiring Wendy Hollo as project coordinator, Debbie Marshall as book editor, and Yvonne DuBourdieu as photographer. Yvonne was also hired to create a film based on a number of the people profiled in the book.

During the development of this anthology, editor Debbie Marshall was privileged to work with some of Alberta's best-loved authors and editors. Despite busy schedules, each of these writers gave unstintingly of his or her time. Every profile required many interviews and long hours of writing. Yet all the writers were eager to participate in the project. Many later commented on the transformative affect that their assignments had on them.

Not all the pieces in this anthology are profiles. Edmonton's poet laureate, Alice Major, contributed our opening poem. It perfectly captures the mood and intent of this book. Gary MacPherson, a long-time advocate for the disabled, graciously provided us with an inspiring preface.

Big Enough Dreams was also strengthened by those who assisted with the book in its final stages of development. Heather Marshall did the final copy edit for the book. In addition to catching mistakes that would have otherwise been missed, she provided useful editorial input. Davey Thompson provided us with the cover art that caught the spirit of "Big Enough Dreams." Our book designer, Jackie Boyko, patiently waited for us to give her the final text and then created the beautiful layout you now have in your hands.

Every book has to have funding in order for writers, editors, photographers, designers, and printers to be paid. Funding for the project was generously provided by a Community Capacity Building Grant from the Edmonton Persons with Developmental Disabilities (PDD) Community Board. It is their hope, and ours, that this book will be a catalyst to help others achieve their own "big enough dreams."